50 French Pizza Recipes for Home

By: Kelly Johnson

Table of Contents

- Classic Margherita with French Mozzarella
- Ratatouille Pizza
- French Onion Soup Pizza
- Croque Madame Pizza
- Provencal Pissaladiere Pizza
- Quiche Lorraine Pizza
- Coq au Vin Pizza
- Duck Confit and Fig Pizza
- French Brie and Pear Pizza
- Smoked Salmon and Crème Fraîche Pizza
- Escargot and Garlic Butter Pizza
- Bouillabaisse Seafood Pizza
- Roquefort and Walnut Pizza
- Camembert and Apple Pizza
- Boeuf Bourguignon Pizza
- Chicken Dijon and Mushroom Pizza
- Nicoise Salad Pizza
- French Tartiflette Pizza
- Gruyere and Caramelized Onion Pizza
- Provençal Chicken and Olive Pizza
- Gratin Dauphinois Pizza
- Tarte Tatin-inspired Apple and Goat Cheese Pizza
- Alsace Flammekueche Pizza
- Salmon and Leek Quiche Pizza
- French Blue Cheese and Pear Pizza
- Croissant Crust Breakfast Pizza
- Pâté and Cornichon Pizza
- Spinach and Gruyere Soufflé Pizza
- Coq au Vin Blanc Pizza
- French Ham and Gouda Pizza
- Mushroom and Gruyere Galette Pizza
- French Lentil and Sausage Pizza
- Gougères (Cheese Puffs) Pizza
- Basque Piquillos and Chorizo Pizza
- French-inspired Duck Sausage Pizza

- Comté Cheese and Potato Pizza
- Salmon Rillettes and Cucumber Pizza
- Leek and Bacon Quiche Pizza
- Pissaladière with Anchovies and Olives Pizza
- French Herb and Goat Cheese Pizza
- Alsace Onion and Bacon Tart Pizza
- Chicken Liver Pâté and Fig Pizza
- French Ratatouille and Goat Cheese Pizza
- Blue Cheese and Caramelized Pear Pizza
- French Tarragon Chicken Pizza
- Garlic Butter Escargot and Mushroom Pizza
- Caramelized Shallot and Thyme Pizza
- French Raclette and Potato Pizza
- Spinach and Roquefort Cheese Pizza
- Alsace Bacon and Onion Flan Pizza

Classic Margherita with French Mozzarella

Ingredients:

For the Pizza Dough:

- 1 pound pizza dough (homemade or store-bought)
- Cornmeal or flour for dusting

For the Margherita Toppings:

- 1 cup French Mozzarella cheese, shredded
- 2 large tomatoes, thinly sliced
- Fresh basil leaves
- Extra virgin olive oil for drizzling
- Salt and black pepper to taste

For the Tomato Sauce:

- 1 cup crushed tomatoes
- 2 cloves garlic, minced
- 1 tablespoon olive oil
- Salt and sugar to taste

Instructions:

For the Tomato Sauce:

Prepare the Tomato Sauce:
- In a saucepan, heat olive oil over medium heat.
- Add minced garlic and sauté until fragrant.
- Pour in crushed tomatoes, season with salt and a pinch of sugar. Simmer for 15-20 minutes until the sauce thickens.
- Remove from heat and let it cool.

For the Margherita Pizza:

Preheat the Oven:
- Preheat your oven to the highest temperature it can go (usually around 475-500°F or 245-260°C).

Prepare the Dough:
- Sprinkle cornmeal or flour on a pizza stone or a baking sheet. Place the rolled-out pizza dough on the prepared surface.

Spread Tomato Sauce:
- Spread a thin layer of the prepared tomato sauce over the pizza dough, leaving a border around the edges for the crust.

Add French Mozzarella:
- Sprinkle the shredded French Mozzarella evenly over the tomato sauce.

Arrange Tomato Slices:
- Arrange the thinly sliced tomatoes over the mozzarella.

Bake the Pizza:
- Place the pizza in the preheated oven and bake for 12-15 minutes or until the crust is golden, and the cheese is melted and bubbly.

Finish and Garnish:
- Remove the Margherita Pizza from the oven. Scatter fresh basil leaves over the hot pizza.

Drizzle with Olive Oil:
- Drizzle extra virgin olive oil over the top of the pizza.

Season with Salt and Pepper:
- Season the pizza with salt and black pepper to taste.

Slice and Serve:
- Allow the pizza to cool for a few minutes before slicing. Serve and enjoy your Classic Margherita Pizza with French Mozzarella!

This classic Margherita pizza with French Mozzarella offers a simple yet exquisite flavor profile, highlighting the freshness of tomatoes, the creaminess of mozzarella, and the aromatic touch of basil. Bon appétit!

Ratatouille Pizza

Ingredients:

For the Ratatouille:

- 1 medium eggplant, diced
- 1 medium zucchini, diced
- 1 red bell pepper, diced
- 1 yellow bell pepper, diced
- 1 onion, finely chopped
- 2 cloves garlic, minced
- 2 tomatoes, diced
- 2 tablespoons tomato paste
- 1 teaspoon dried thyme
- 1 teaspoon dried rosemary
- Salt and black pepper to taste
- Olive oil for cooking

For the Pizza:

- 1 pound pizza dough (homemade or store-bought)
- Olive oil for brushing
- 1 cup shredded mozzarella cheese
- Fresh basil leaves for garnish

Instructions:

For the Ratatouille:

Prepare the Vegetables:
- In a large skillet, heat olive oil over medium heat. Add the chopped onion and garlic, sautéing until softened.

Cook the Eggplant and Zucchini:
- Add the diced eggplant and zucchini to the skillet. Cook until they start to brown.

Add Bell Peppers and Tomatoes:

- Stir in the diced red and yellow bell peppers, and diced tomatoes.

Season and Simmer:

- Add tomato paste, dried thyme, dried rosemary, salt, and black pepper. Mix well and let the ratatouille simmer until the vegetables are tender and the flavors meld together. This may take around 15-20 minutes.

For the Pizza:

Preheat the Oven:

- Preheat your oven to the highest temperature it can go (usually around 475-500°F or 245-260°C).

Prepare the Dough:

- Roll out the pizza dough onto a baking sheet or pizza stone.

Brush with Olive Oil:

- Brush the surface of the dough with olive oil.

Spread Ratatouille:

- Spread a generous amount of the prepared ratatouille over the pizza dough, leaving a border for the crust.

Add Mozzarella Cheese:

- Sprinkle shredded mozzarella cheese evenly over the ratatouille.

Bake the Pizza:

- Place the pizza in the preheated oven and bake for 12-15 minutes, or until the crust is golden and the cheese is melted and bubbly.

Finish and Garnish:

- Remove the Ratatouille Pizza from the oven. Garnish with fresh basil leaves.

Slice and Serve:

- Allow the pizza to cool for a few minutes before slicing. Serve and enjoy your delicious Ratatouille Pizza!

This pizza brings together the classic French flavors of ratatouille with the comfort of a pizza. It's a perfect way to enjoy the traditional Provencal vegetable stew in a new and delightful form. Enjoy!

French Onion Soup Pizza

Ingredients:

For the Caramelized Onions:

- 4 large yellow onions, thinly sliced
- 2 tablespoons unsalted butter
- 2 tablespoons olive oil
- 1 teaspoon sugar
- Salt and black pepper to taste
- 1/4 cup beef broth (optional)

For the Pizza:

- 1 pound pizza dough (homemade or store-bought)
- 1 cup shredded Gruyere cheese
- 1 cup shredded mozzarella cheese
- 1/4 cup Parmesan cheese, grated
- Fresh thyme leaves for garnish
- Balsamic glaze for drizzling (optional)

Instructions:

For the Caramelized Onions:

Caramelize the Onions:
- In a large skillet, heat butter and olive oil over medium heat. Add the thinly sliced onions and sugar. Stir to coat the onions.
- Cook the onions, stirring occasionally, until they become golden brown and caramelized. This process may take around 20-30 minutes.
- If the onions start to stick, you can add a bit of beef broth to deglaze the pan and add extra flavor.
- Season the caramelized onions with salt and black pepper. Set aside.

For the Pizza:

Preheat the Oven:
- Preheat your oven to the highest temperature it can go (usually around 475-500°F or 245-260°C).

Prepare the Dough:
- Roll out the pizza dough onto a baking sheet or pizza stone.

Spread Caramelized Onions:
- Spread the caramelized onions evenly over the pizza dough, leaving a border for the crust.

Add Cheese:
- Sprinkle a combination of shredded Gruyere, mozzarella, and Parmesan cheese over the caramelized onions.

Bake the Pizza:
- Place the pizza in the preheated oven and bake for 12-15 minutes, or until the crust is golden and the cheese is melted and bubbly.

Finish and Garnish:
- Remove the French Onion Soup Pizza from the oven. Sprinkle fresh thyme leaves over the hot pizza.
- If desired, drizzle with balsamic glaze for an extra layer of flavor.

Slice and Serve:
- Allow the pizza to cool for a few minutes before slicing. Serve and enjoy your savory French Onion Soup Pizza!

This pizza captures the rich and savory flavors of French onion soup, making it a delightful and comforting twist on a classic dish. Bon appétit!

Croque Madame Pizza

Ingredients:

For the Béchamel Sauce:

- 2 tablespoons unsalted butter
- 2 tablespoons all-purpose flour
- 1 cup milk
- Salt, pepper, and nutmeg to taste

For the Pizza:

- 1 pound pizza dough (homemade or store-bought)
- 1 cup shredded Gruyere cheese
- 1 cup cooked ham, thinly sliced
- 4 eggs
- Salt and black pepper to taste
- Chopped fresh parsley for garnish

Instructions:

For the Béchamel Sauce:

Prepare the Béchamel:
- In a saucepan, melt the butter over medium heat. Add the flour and whisk continuously to create a roux.
- Slowly pour in the milk while whisking constantly to avoid lumps. Continue to whisk until the mixture thickens.
- Season the béchamel with salt, pepper, and a pinch of nutmeg. Remove from heat and set aside.

For the Pizza:

Preheat the Oven:
- Preheat your oven to the highest temperature it can go (usually around 475-500°F or 245-260°C).

Prepare the Dough:
- Roll out the pizza dough onto a baking sheet or pizza stone.

Spread Béchamel Sauce:
- Spread a generous layer of the prepared béchamel sauce over the pizza dough, leaving a border for the crust.

Add Cheese and Ham:
- Sprinkle shredded Gruyere cheese evenly over the béchamel. Place the thinly sliced ham over the cheese.

Crack and Add Eggs:
- Carefully crack the eggs onto the pizza, distributing them evenly.

Season and Bake:
- Season the eggs with salt and black pepper. Place the pizza in the preheated oven and bake for 12-15 minutes, or until the crust is golden, the cheese is melted, and the eggs are cooked to your liking.

Finish and Garnish:
- Remove the Croque Madame Pizza from the oven. Garnish with chopped fresh parsley.

Slice and Serve:
- Allow the pizza to cool for a few minutes before slicing. Serve and enjoy your delightful Croque Madame Pizza!

This pizza puts a delicious spin on the classic Croque Madame sandwich by transforming it into a delightful pizza. The combination of creamy béchamel, Gruyere cheese, ham, and a perfectly cooked egg on top creates a savory and satisfying dish. Bon appétit!

Provencal Pissaladiere Pizza

Ingredients:

For the Pizza Dough:

- 1 pound pizza dough (homemade or store-bought)
- Olive oil for brushing

For the Topping:

- 2 tablespoons olive oil
- 4 large yellow onions, thinly sliced
- 2 cloves garlic, minced
- 1 teaspoon dried thyme
- 1 teaspoon dried rosemary
- Salt and black pepper to taste
- 1 cup Niçoise olives, pitted
- 6-8 anchovy fillets
- Fresh thyme leaves for garnish

Instructions:

For the Pizza Dough:

Prepare the Dough:
- Roll out the pizza dough onto a baking sheet or pizza stone. If using a pizza stone, make sure it is preheated in the oven.

Brush with Olive Oil:
- Brush the surface of the dough with olive oil.

For the Topping:

Caramelize the Onions:
- In a large skillet, heat 2 tablespoons of olive oil over medium heat. Add the thinly sliced onions, minced garlic, dried thyme, dried rosemary, salt, and black pepper.
- Cook the onions, stirring occasionally, until they become golden brown and caramelized. This process may take around 20-30 minutes.

Preheat the Oven:

- Preheat your oven to the highest temperature it can go (usually around 475-500°F or 245-260°C).

Assemble the Pissaladière:
- Spread the caramelized onions evenly over the pizza dough, leaving a border for the crust.
- Arrange Niçoise olives and anchovy fillets on top of the caramelized onions.

Bake the Pizza:
- Place the pizza in the preheated oven and bake for 12-15 minutes, or until the crust is golden and the toppings are heated through.

Finish and Garnish:
- Remove the Provencal Pissaladière Pizza from the oven. Garnish with fresh thyme leaves.

Slice and Serve:
- Allow the pizza to cool for a few minutes before slicing. Serve and enjoy your flavorful Provencal Pissaladière Pizza!

This pizza celebrates the flavors of Provence with sweet caramelized onions, briny Niçoise olives, and savory anchovies. The combination of these classic ingredients makes for a delicious and authentic Pissaladière experience. Bon appétit!

Quiche Lorraine Pizza

Ingredients:

For the Pizza Dough:

- 1 pound pizza dough (homemade or store-bought)
- Olive oil for brushing

For the Quiche Lorraine Topping:

- 1 cup heavy cream
- 3 large eggs
- 1 cup shredded Gruyere cheese
- 1 cup diced cooked bacon or lardons
- Salt and black pepper to taste
- Fresh chives for garnish (optional)

Instructions:

For the Pizza Dough:

Prepare the Dough:
- Roll out the pizza dough onto a baking sheet or pizza stone. If using a pizza stone, make sure it is preheated in the oven.

Brush with Olive Oil:
- Brush the surface of the dough with olive oil.

For the Quiche Lorraine Topping:

Preheat the Oven:
- Preheat your oven to the highest temperature it can go (usually around 475-500°F or 245-260°C).

Prepare the Quiche Filling:
- In a bowl, whisk together the heavy cream and eggs until well combined. Stir in the shredded Gruyere cheese and diced cooked bacon. Season with salt and black pepper to taste.

Assemble the Quiche Lorraine Pizza:
- Spread the quiche filling evenly over the pizza dough, leaving a border for the crust.

Bake the Pizza:
- Place the pizza in the preheated oven and bake for 12-15 minutes, or until the crust is golden, and the quiche filling is set and slightly golden on top.

Finish and Garnish:
- Remove the Quiche Lorraine Pizza from the oven. Garnish with fresh chives if desired.

Slice and Serve:
- Allow the pizza to cool for a few minutes before slicing. Serve and enjoy your delicious Quiche Lorraine Pizza!

This pizza combines the classic flavors of Quiche Lorraine – the creamy custard filling, Gruyere cheese, and savory bacon – with the convenience and deliciousness of pizza.

It's a perfect blend of two beloved dishes. Bon appétit!

Coq au Vin Pizza

Ingredients:

For the Pizza Dough:

- 1 pound pizza dough (homemade or store-bought)
- Olive oil for brushing

For the Coq au Vin Topping:

- 2 tablespoons olive oil
- 4 boneless, skinless chicken thighs, cut into bite-sized pieces
- Salt and black pepper to taste
- 1 cup red wine
- 1 cup chicken broth
- 2 tablespoons tomato paste
- 2 cloves garlic, minced
- 1 onion, finely chopped
- 8 ounces mushrooms, sliced
- 2 tablespoons all-purpose flour
- Fresh thyme leaves for garnish
- Grated Gruyere cheese for topping

Instructions:

For the Pizza Dough:

Prepare the Dough:
- Roll out the pizza dough onto a baking sheet or pizza stone. If using a pizza stone, make sure it is preheated in the oven.

Brush with Olive Oil:
- Brush the surface of the dough with olive oil.

For the Coq au Vin Topping:

Preheat the Oven:

- Preheat your oven to the highest temperature it can go (usually around 475-500°F or 245-260°C).

Cook the Chicken:
- In a skillet, heat olive oil over medium heat. Season the chicken thighs with salt and black pepper, then brown them in the hot oil.

Prepare the Coq au Vin Sauce:
- Add minced garlic and chopped onions to the skillet. Cook until the onions are translucent.
- Sprinkle flour over the chicken and onions, stirring to create a roux.
- Pour in the red wine, chicken broth, and add tomato paste. Stir to combine and bring to a simmer. Cook until the sauce thickens.
- Add sliced mushrooms and continue cooking until the chicken is cooked through and the mushrooms are tender. Adjust seasoning if needed.

Assemble the Coq au Vin Pizza:
- Spread the prepared Coq au Vin mixture evenly over the pizza dough, leaving a border for the crust.

Bake the Pizza:
- Place the pizza in the preheated oven and bake for 12-15 minutes, or until the crust is golden, and the toppings are heated through.

Finish and Garnish:
- Remove the Coq au Vin Pizza from the oven. Sprinkle grated Gruyere cheese over the hot pizza.
- Garnish with fresh thyme leaves.

Slice and Serve:
- Allow the pizza to cool for a few minutes before slicing. Serve and enjoy your savory Coq au Vin Pizza!

This pizza takes inspiration from the classic French dish, Coq au Vin, and transforms it into a unique and delicious pizza experience. Bon appétit!

Duck Confit and Fig Pizza

Ingredients:

For the Pizza Dough:

- 1 pound pizza dough (homemade or store-bought)
- Olive oil for brushing

For the Duck Confit and Fig Topping:

- 2 duck confit legs, shredded
- 1 cup fig jam or preserves
- 1 cup fresh figs, sliced
- 1 cup arugula
- 1 cup goat cheese, crumbled
- Balsamic glaze for drizzling
- Salt and black pepper to taste

Instructions:

For the Pizza Dough:

Prepare the Dough:
- Roll out the pizza dough onto a baking sheet or pizza stone. If using a pizza stone, make sure it is preheated in the oven.

Brush with Olive Oil:
- Brush the surface of the dough with olive oil.

For the Duck Confit and Fig Topping:

Preheat the Oven:
- Preheat your oven to the highest temperature it can go (usually around 475-500°F or 245-260°C).

Assemble the Pizza:
- Spread a generous layer of fig jam over the pizza dough, leaving a border for the crust.
- Distribute the shredded duck confit evenly over the fig jam.
- Scatter sliced fresh figs and crumbled goat cheese over the pizza.

Season and Bake:

- Season the pizza with salt and black pepper to taste. Place the pizza in the preheated oven and bake for 12-15 minutes, or until the crust is golden, and the toppings are heated through.

Finish and Garnish:
- Remove the Duck Confit and Fig Pizza from the oven. Drizzle balsamic glaze over the hot pizza.
- Top with fresh arugula for a peppery and vibrant finish.

Slice and Serve:
- Allow the pizza to cool for a few minutes before slicing. Serve and enjoy your luxurious Duck Confit and Fig Pizza!

This pizza combines the rich and savory flavors of duck confit with the sweetness of figs and the creaminess of goat cheese, creating a gourmet pizza experience. The balsamic glaze and arugula add a perfect balance to the dish. Bon appétit!

French Brie and Pear Pizza

Ingredients:

For the Pizza Dough:

- 1 pound pizza dough (homemade or store-bought)
- Olive oil for brushing

For the Brie and Pear Topping:

- 1 medium-sized ripe pear, thinly sliced
- 6 ounces Brie cheese, thinly sliced
- 1/4 cup chopped walnuts
- 2 tablespoons honey
- Fresh thyme leaves for garnish
- Salt and black pepper to taste

Instructions:

For the Pizza Dough:

Prepare the Dough:
- Roll out the pizza dough onto a baking sheet or pizza stone. If using a pizza stone, make sure it is preheated in the oven.

Brush with Olive Oil:
- Brush the surface of the dough with olive oil.

For the Brie and Pear Topping:

Preheat the Oven:
- Preheat your oven to the highest temperature it can go (usually around 475-500°F or 245-260°C).

Assemble the Pizza:
- Arrange the thinly sliced pears evenly over the pizza dough, leaving a border for the crust.
- Place the thinly sliced Brie cheese on top of the pears.
- Sprinkle chopped walnuts over the pizza.

Season and Bake:

- Season the pizza with salt and black pepper to taste. Place the pizza in the preheated oven and bake for 12-15 minutes, or until the crust is golden, and the toppings are heated through.

Finish and Garnish:
- Remove the Brie and Pear Pizza from the oven. Drizzle honey over the hot pizza.
- Garnish with fresh thyme leaves for a fragrant and herbaceous touch.

Slice and Serve:
- Allow the pizza to cool for a few minutes before slicing. Serve and enjoy your elegant Brie and Pear Pizza!

This pizza combines the creamy richness of Brie cheese with the sweetness of ripe pears, creating a sophisticated and delicious flavor profile. The addition of honey and thyme adds an extra layer of complexity to the dish. Bon appétit!

Smoked Salmon and Crème Fraîche Pizza

Ingredients:

For the Pizza Dough:

- 1 pound pizza dough (homemade or store-bought)
- Olive oil for brushing

For the Smoked Salmon and Crème Fraîche Topping:

- 1/2 cup crème fraîche
- 8 ounces smoked salmon, thinly sliced
- 1 small red onion, thinly sliced
- Capers for topping
- Fresh dill, chopped, for garnish
- Lemon wedges for serving
- Salt and black pepper to taste

Instructions:

For the Pizza Dough:

Prepare the Dough:
- Roll out the pizza dough onto a baking sheet or pizza stone. If using a pizza stone, make sure it is preheated in the oven.

Brush with Olive Oil:
- Brush the surface of the dough with olive oil.

For the Smoked Salmon and Crème Fraîche Topping:

Preheat the Oven:
- Preheat your oven to the highest temperature it can go (usually around 475-500°F or 245-260°C).

Assemble the Pizza:
- Spread crème fraîche evenly over the pizza dough, leaving a border for the crust.

- Arrange thinly sliced smoked salmon and red onion over the crème fraîche.
- Sprinkle capers over the pizza.

Season and Bake:
- Season the pizza with salt and black pepper to taste. Place the pizza in the preheated oven and bake for 12-15 minutes, or until the crust is golden, and the toppings are heated through.

Finish and Garnish:
- Remove the Smoked Salmon and Crème Fraîche Pizza from the oven. Sprinkle chopped fresh dill over the hot pizza.

Slice and Serve:
- Allow the pizza to cool for a few minutes before slicing. Serve with lemon wedges on the side for a fresh and zesty touch.

This pizza showcases the luxurious combination of smoked salmon and creamy crème fraîche, making it a perfect dish for a special occasion or a gourmet pizza night. The addition of capers and fresh dill adds a burst of flavor. Enjoy!

Escargot and Garlic Butter Pizza

Ingredients:

For the Pizza Dough:

- 1 pound pizza dough (homemade or store-bought)
- Olive oil for brushing

For the Escargot and Garlic Butter Topping:

- 1 can (about 7 ounces) of escargot, drained and rinsed
- 1/2 cup unsalted butter, softened
- 4 cloves garlic, minced
- 2 tablespoons fresh parsley, finely chopped
- Salt and black pepper to taste
- Grated Parmesan cheese for topping
- Lemon wedges for serving (optional)

Instructions:

For the Pizza Dough:

Prepare the Dough:
- Roll out the pizza dough onto a baking sheet or pizza stone. If using a pizza stone, make sure it is preheated in the oven.

Brush with Olive Oil:
- Brush the surface of the dough with olive oil.

For the Escargot and Garlic Butter Topping:

Preheat the Oven:
- Preheat your oven to the highest temperature it can go (usually around 475-500°F or 245-260°C).

Prepare the Garlic Butter:
- In a bowl, combine the softened butter, minced garlic, chopped parsley, salt, and black pepper. Mix well to create a garlic butter spread.

Assemble the Pizza:
- Spread a generous layer of the garlic butter mixture evenly over the pizza dough, leaving a border for the crust.

- Arrange the drained and rinsed escargot evenly over the garlic butter.

Bake the Pizza:
- Place the pizza in the preheated oven and bake for 12-15 minutes, or until the crust is golden, and the toppings are heated through.

Finish and Garnish:
- Remove the Escargot and Garlic Butter Pizza from the oven. Sprinkle grated Parmesan cheese over the hot pizza.

Serve:
- Allow the pizza to cool for a few minutes before slicing. Serve with lemon wedges on the side for a citrusy touch.

This pizza brings together the rich and buttery flavors of escargot with the aromatic goodness of garlic butter. It's a unique and indulgent dish that is sure to delight adventurous taste buds. Enjoy!

Bouillabaisse Seafood Pizza

Ingredients:

For the Pizza Dough:

- 1 pound pizza dough (homemade or store-bought)
- Olive oil for brushing

For the Bouillabaisse Seafood Topping:

- 1/2 cup tomato sauce or marinara sauce
- 1/2 cup fish or seafood broth
- 1/2 teaspoon saffron threads (optional)
- 1 teaspoon fennel seeds
- 1 clove garlic, minced
- 1/2 cup diced tomatoes
- 1/2 cup cooked and mixed seafood (shrimp, mussels, clams, squid, etc.)
- 1/4 cup black olives, pitted and sliced
- 2 tablespoons capers
- Fresh parsley, chopped, for garnish
- Lemon wedges for serving

Instructions:

For the Pizza Dough:

> Prepare the Dough:
> - Roll out the pizza dough onto a baking sheet or pizza stone. If using a pizza stone, make sure it is preheated in the oven.
>
> Brush with Olive Oil:
> - Brush the surface of the dough with olive oil.

For the Bouillabaisse Seafood Topping:

> Preheat the Oven:
> - Preheat your oven to the highest temperature it can go (usually around 475-500°F or 245-260°C).
>
> Prepare the Bouillabaisse Sauce:

- In a small saucepan, combine the tomato sauce, fish or seafood broth, saffron threads (if using), fennel seeds, and minced garlic. Simmer over low heat for about 10 minutes to infuse the flavors. Remove from heat.

Assemble the Pizza:
- Spread the bouillabaisse sauce evenly over the pizza dough, leaving a border for the crust.
- Sprinkle diced tomatoes, mixed seafood, black olives, and capers over the pizza.

Bake the Pizza:
- Place the pizza in the preheated oven and bake for 12-15 minutes, or until the crust is golden, and the seafood is cooked through.

Finish and Garnish:
- Remove the Bouillabaisse Seafood Pizza from the oven. Sprinkle chopped fresh parsley over the hot pizza.

Serve:
- Allow the pizza to cool for a few minutes before slicing. Serve with lemon wedges on the side for a burst of citrus flavor.

This pizza captures the essence of the classic French seafood stew, bouillabaisse, with a creative twist. The combination of saffron-infused sauce and a medley of fresh seafood creates a flavorful and satisfying dish. Enjoy!

Roquefort and Walnut Pizza

Ingredients:

For the Pizza Dough:

- 1 pound pizza dough (homemade or store-bought)
- Olive oil for brushing

For the Roquefort and Walnut Topping:

- 1/2 cup crumbled Roquefort or blue cheese
- 1/2 cup chopped walnuts
- 1 tablespoon honey
- 2 tablespoons balsamic glaze
- Fresh thyme leaves for garnish
- Salt and black pepper to taste

Instructions:

For the Pizza Dough:

> Prepare the Dough:
> - Roll out the pizza dough onto a baking sheet or pizza stone. If using a pizza stone, make sure it is preheated in the oven.
>
> Brush with Olive Oil:
> - Brush the surface of the dough with olive oil.

For the Roquefort and Walnut Topping:

> Preheat the Oven:
> - Preheat your oven to the highest temperature it can go (usually around 475-500°F or 245-260°C).
>
> Assemble the Pizza:
> - Sprinkle crumbled Roquefort or blue cheese evenly over the pizza dough, leaving a border for the crust.
> - Scatter chopped walnuts over the cheese.
>
> Drizzle with Honey and Balsamic Glaze:
> - Drizzle honey and balsamic glaze over the pizza.
>
> Season and Bake:

- Season the pizza with salt and black pepper to taste. Place the pizza in the preheated oven and bake for 12-15 minutes, or until the crust is golden, and the toppings are heated through.

Finish and Garnish:
- Remove the Roquefort and Walnut Pizza from the oven. Sprinkle fresh thyme leaves over the hot pizza.

Slice and Serve:
- Allow the pizza to cool for a few minutes before slicing. Serve and enjoy your sophisticated Roquefort and Walnut Pizza!

This pizza combines the bold flavors of Roquefort cheese with the nuttiness of walnuts and the sweetness of honey and balsamic glaze. The result is a gourmet pizza that's perfect for those who appreciate rich and savory taste experiences. Bon appétit!

Camembert and Apple Pizza

Ingredients:

For the Pizza Dough:

- 1 pound pizza dough (homemade or store-bought)
- Olive oil for brushing

For the Camembert and Apple Topping:

- 1 round Camembert cheese, sliced
- 1-2 apples, thinly sliced (use a sweet variety like Honeycrisp or Gala)
- 1/4 cup chopped walnuts
- 2 tablespoons honey
- Fresh thyme leaves for garnish
- Salt and black pepper to taste

Instructions:

For the Pizza Dough:

Prepare the Dough:
- Roll out the pizza dough onto a baking sheet or pizza stone. If using a pizza stone, make sure it is preheated in the oven.

Brush with Olive Oil:
- Brush the surface of the dough with olive oil.

For the Camembert and Apple Topping:

Preheat the Oven:
- Preheat your oven to the highest temperature it can go (usually around 475-500°F or 245-260°C).

Assemble the Pizza:
- Arrange sliced Camembert cheese evenly over the pizza dough, leaving a border for the crust.
- Place thinly sliced apples on top of the Camembert.
- Sprinkle chopped walnuts over the pizza.

Drizzle with Honey:
- Drizzle honey over the pizza.

Season and Bake:
- Season the pizza with salt and black pepper to taste. Place the pizza in the preheated oven and bake for 12-15 minutes, or until the crust is golden, and the toppings are heated through.

Finish and Garnish:
- Remove the Camembert and Apple Pizza from the oven. Sprinkle fresh thyme leaves over the hot pizza.

Slice and Serve:
- Allow the pizza to cool for a few minutes before slicing. Serve and enjoy your delightful Camembert and Apple Pizza!

This pizza combines the creamy and savory notes of Camembert cheese with the sweetness of thinly sliced apples, creating a delicious balance of flavors. The addition of honey and thyme adds a touch of sophistication to this gourmet pizza. Bon appétit!

Boeuf Bourguignon Pizza

Ingredients:

For the Pizza Dough:

- 1 pound pizza dough (homemade or store-bought)
- Olive oil for brushing

For the Boeuf Bourguignon Topping:

- 1 cup leftover Boeuf Bourguignon (beef stewed in red wine)
- 1 cup shredded Gruyere cheese
- 1/2 cup caramelized onions
- Fresh thyme leaves for garnish
- Salt and black pepper to taste

Instructions:

For the Pizza Dough:

Prepare the Dough:
- Roll out the pizza dough onto a baking sheet or pizza stone. If using a pizza stone, make sure it is preheated in the oven.

Brush with Olive Oil:
- Brush the surface of the dough with olive oil.

For the Boeuf Bourguignon Topping:

Preheat the Oven:
- Preheat your oven to the highest temperature it can go (usually around 475-500°F or 245-260°C).

Assemble the Pizza:
- Spread leftover Boeuf Bourguignon evenly over the pizza dough, leaving a border for the crust.
- Sprinkle shredded Gruyere cheese over the Boeuf Bourguignon.
- Distribute caramelized onions over the pizza.

Season and Bake:
- Season the pizza with salt and black pepper to taste. Place the pizza in the preheated oven and bake for 12-15 minutes, or until the crust is golden, and the toppings are heated through.

Finish and Garnish:
- Remove the Boeuf Bourguignon Pizza from the oven. Sprinkle fresh thyme leaves over the hot pizza.

Slice and Serve:
- Allow the pizza to cool for a few minutes before slicing. Serve and enjoy your unique Boeuf Bourguignon Pizza!

This pizza takes inspiration from the classic French dish, Boeuf Bourguignon, transforming it into a creative and savory pizza. The rich flavors of the beef stew, combined with Gruyere cheese and caramelized onions, make for a delicious and hearty meal. Bon appétit!

Chicken Dijon and Mushroom Pizza

Ingredients:

For the Pizza Dough:

- 1 pound pizza dough (homemade or store-bought)
- Olive oil for brushing

For the Chicken Dijon and Mushroom Topping:

- 1 cup cooked and shredded chicken breast
- 1/2 cup Dijon mustard
- 1 cup sliced mushrooms (use your favorite variety)
- 1 cup shredded mozzarella cheese
- 1/2 cup grated Parmesan cheese
- 2 cloves garlic, minced
- Fresh thyme leaves for garnish
- Salt and black pepper to taste

Instructions:

For the Pizza Dough:

Prepare the Dough:
- Roll out the pizza dough onto a baking sheet or pizza stone. If using a pizza stone, make sure it is preheated in the oven.

Brush with Olive Oil:
- Brush the surface of the dough with olive oil.

For the Chicken Dijon and Mushroom Topping:

Preheat the Oven:
- Preheat your oven to the highest temperature it can go (usually around 475-500°F or 245-260°C).

Assemble the Pizza:
- Spread Dijon mustard evenly over the pizza dough, leaving a border for the crust.
- Distribute cooked and shredded chicken over the mustard.
- Scatter sliced mushrooms and minced garlic over the pizza.

- Sprinkle shredded mozzarella and grated Parmesan cheese over the toppings.

Season and Bake:
- Season the pizza with salt and black pepper to taste. Place the pizza in the preheated oven and bake for 12-15 minutes, or until the crust is golden, and the toppings are heated through.

Finish and Garnish:
- Remove the Chicken Dijon and Mushroom Pizza from the oven. Sprinkle fresh thyme leaves over the hot pizza.

Slice and Serve:
- Allow the pizza to cool for a few minutes before slicing. Serve and enjoy your flavorful Chicken Dijon and Mushroom Pizza!

This pizza combines the tangy kick of Dijon mustard with savory chicken, earthy mushrooms, and melted cheeses, creating a delightful and gourmet flavor profile. The addition of fresh thyme adds a fragrant touch. Bon appétit!

Nicoise Salad Pizza

Ingredients:

For the Pizza Dough:

- 1 pound pizza dough (homemade or store-bought)
- Olive oil for brushing

For the Niçoise Salad Topping:

- 1/2 cup prepared basil pesto
- 1 cup cherry tomatoes, halved
- 1/2 cup Kalamata olives, pitted and sliced
- 1/2 cup green beans, blanched and sliced
- 1/2 cup red bell pepper, thinly sliced
- 1/4 cup red onion, thinly sliced
- 1/2 cup canned tuna, drained and flaked
- 2 hard-boiled eggs, sliced
- Fresh basil leaves for garnish
- Salt and black pepper to taste

Instructions:

For the Pizza Dough:

Prepare the Dough:
- Roll out the pizza dough onto a baking sheet or pizza stone. If using a pizza stone, make sure it is preheated in the oven.

Brush with Olive Oil:
- Brush the surface of the dough with olive oil.

For the Niçoise Salad Topping:

Preheat the Oven:
- Preheat your oven to the highest temperature it can go (usually around 475-500°F or 245-260°C).

Assemble the Pizza:
- Spread a layer of basil pesto evenly over the pizza dough, leaving a border for the crust.

- Arrange halved cherry tomatoes, sliced olives, blanched and sliced green beans, sliced red bell pepper, and thinly sliced red onion over the pesto.
- Distribute flaked tuna and sliced hard-boiled eggs on top.

Season and Bake:
- Season the pizza with salt and black pepper to taste. Place the pizza in the preheated oven and bake for 12-15 minutes, or until the crust is golden, and the toppings are heated through.

Finish and Garnish:
- Remove the Niçoise Salad Pizza from the oven. Sprinkle fresh basil leaves over the hot pizza.

Slice and Serve:
- Allow the pizza to cool for a few minutes before slicing. Serve and enjoy your Niçoise Salad-inspired Pizza!

This pizza captures the flavors of the classic Niçoise Salad, featuring vibrant and fresh ingredients like cherry tomatoes, olives, green beans, tuna, and more. The basil pesto adds a burst of herbaceous goodness. It's a delightful and refreshing pizza option. Bon appétit!

French Tartiflette Pizza

Ingredients:

For the Pizza Dough:

- 1 pound pizza dough (homemade or store-bought)
- Olive oil for brushing

For the Tartiflette Topping:

- 1 1/2 pounds Yukon Gold potatoes, thinly sliced
- 1 tablespoon olive oil
- 1 large onion, thinly sliced
- 8 ounces bacon, diced
- 1 cup Reblochon cheese, diced (substitute with Gruyere or Brie if unavailable)
- 1/2 cup sour cream
- Salt and black pepper to taste
- Fresh chives, chopped, for garnish

Instructions:

For the Pizza Dough:

Prepare the Dough:
- Roll out the pizza dough onto a baking sheet or pizza stone. If using a pizza stone, make sure it is preheated in the oven.

Brush with Olive Oil:
- Brush the surface of the dough with olive oil.

For the Tartiflette Topping:

Preheat the Oven:
- Preheat your oven to the highest temperature it can go (usually around 475-500°F or 245-260°C).

Cook the Potatoes:

- Place the thinly sliced potatoes in a pot of salted boiling water and cook for about 5 minutes, just until they are slightly tender. Drain and set aside.

Sauté Onions and Bacon:
- In a skillet, heat olive oil over medium heat. Add the sliced onions and diced bacon. Cook until the bacon is crispy, and the onions are soft and caramelized.

Assemble the Pizza:
- Spread the sautéed onions and bacon mixture evenly over the pizza dough.
- Arrange the parboiled sliced potatoes on top.
- Sprinkle diced Reblochon cheese over the potatoes.

Add Sour Cream and Season:
- Dot the top of the pizza with spoonfuls of sour cream.
- Season the pizza with salt and black pepper to taste.

Bake the Pizza:
- Place the pizza in the preheated oven and bake for 12-15 minutes, or until the crust is golden, and the toppings are heated through.

Finish and Garnish:
- Remove the Tartiflette Pizza from the oven. Sprinkle chopped fresh chives over the hot pizza.

Slice and Serve:
- Allow the pizza to cool for a few minutes before slicing. Serve and enjoy your French-inspired Tartiflette Pizza!

This pizza takes inspiration from the classic French dish Tartiflette, featuring layers of potatoes, bacon, onions, and creamy cheese. It's a hearty and comforting pizza that brings the flavors of the French Alps to your table. Bon appétit!

Gruyere and Caramelized Onion Pizza

Ingredients:

For the Pizza Dough:

- 1 pound pizza dough (homemade or store-bought)
- Olive oil for brushing

For the Gruyere and Caramelized Onion Topping:

- 2 large onions, thinly sliced
- 2 tablespoons olive oil
- 1 tablespoon balsamic vinegar
- 1 teaspoon sugar
- Salt and black pepper to taste
- 1 1/2 cups shredded Gruyere cheese
- Fresh thyme leaves for garnish (optional)

Instructions:

For the Pizza Dough:

Prepare the Dough:
- Roll out the pizza dough onto a baking sheet or pizza stone. If using a pizza stone, make sure it is preheated in the oven.

Brush with Olive Oil:
- Brush the surface of the dough with olive oil.

For the Gruyere and Caramelized Onion Topping:

Preheat the Oven:
- Preheat your oven to the highest temperature it can go (usually around 475-500°F or 245-260°C).

Caramelize the Onions:
- In a large skillet, heat 2 tablespoons of olive oil over medium-low heat. Add the thinly sliced onions and cook, stirring occasionally, until the onions are soft and golden brown.

- Add balsamic vinegar, sugar, salt, and black pepper to the caramelized onions. Continue cooking for an additional 2-3 minutes. Remove from heat.

Assemble the Pizza:
- Spread the caramelized onions evenly over the pizza dough, leaving a border for the crust.
- Sprinkle shredded Gruyere cheese over the caramelized onions.

Bake the Pizza:
- Place the pizza in the preheated oven and bake for 12-15 minutes, or until the crust is golden, and the cheese is melted and bubbly.

Finish and Garnish:
- Remove the Gruyere and Caramelized Onion Pizza from the oven. Sprinkle fresh thyme leaves over the hot pizza if desired.

Slice and Serve:
- Allow the pizza to cool for a few minutes before slicing. Serve and enjoy your Gruyere and Caramelized Onion Pizza!

This pizza combines the rich and nutty flavor of Gruyere cheese with the sweetness of caramelized onions, creating a delightful balance of savory and sweet. The addition of balsamic vinegar adds a tangy note to enhance the overall taste. Bon appétit!

Provençal Chicken and Olive Pizza

Ingredients:

For the Pizza Dough:

- 1 pound pizza dough (homemade or store-bought)
- Olive oil for brushing

For the Provençal Chicken and Olive Topping:

- 1 cup cooked and shredded chicken breast
- 1/2 cup black olives, sliced
- 1/2 cup cherry tomatoes, halved
- 1/4 cup sun-dried tomatoes, sliced
- 1/4 cup red onion, thinly sliced
- 2 cloves garlic, minced
- 1 teaspoon dried Herbes de Provence
- 1 cup shredded mozzarella cheese
- 1/4 cup grated Parmesan cheese
- Salt and black pepper to taste
- Fresh basil leaves for garnish

Instructions:

For the Pizza Dough:

Prepare the Dough:
- Roll out the pizza dough onto a baking sheet or pizza stone. If using a pizza stone, make sure it is preheated in the oven.

Brush with Olive Oil:
- Brush the surface of the dough with olive oil.

For the Provençal Chicken and Olive Topping:

Preheat the Oven:
- Preheat your oven to the highest temperature it can go (usually around 475-500°F or 245-260°C).

Assemble the Pizza:

- Spread the shredded chicken evenly over the pizza dough, leaving a border for the crust.
- Distribute sliced black olives, halved cherry tomatoes, sliced sun-dried tomatoes, thinly sliced red onion, and minced garlic over the chicken.
- Sprinkle dried Herbes de Provence over the toppings.
- Add shredded mozzarella and grated Parmesan cheese on top.

Season and Bake:
- Season the pizza with salt and black pepper to taste. Place the pizza in the preheated oven and bake for 12-15 minutes, or until the crust is golden, and the toppings are heated through.

Finish and Garnish:
- Remove the Provençal Chicken and Olive Pizza from the oven. Sprinkle fresh basil leaves over the hot pizza.

Slice and Serve:
- Allow the pizza to cool for a few minutes before slicing. Serve and enjoy your Provençal-inspired Chicken and Olive Pizza!

This pizza captures the flavors of the Provençal region with a combination of Mediterranean ingredients. The Herbes de Provence add a fragrant and herby touch to enhance the overall taste. Bon appétit!

Gratin Dauphinois Pizza

Ingredients:

For the Pizza Dough:

- 1 pound pizza dough (homemade or store-bought)
- Olive oil for brushing

For the Gratin Dauphinois Topping:

- 3 large potatoes, peeled and thinly sliced
- 2 cups heavy cream
- 2 garlic cloves, minced
- 1 cup grated Gruyere cheese
- Salt and black pepper to taste
- Fresh thyme leaves for garnish

Instructions:

For the Pizza Dough:

Prepare the Dough:
- Roll out the pizza dough onto a baking sheet or pizza stone. If using a pizza stone, make sure it is preheated in the oven.

Brush with Olive Oil:
- Brush the surface of the dough with olive oil.

For the Gratin Dauphinois Topping:

Preheat the Oven:
- Preheat your oven to the highest temperature it can go (usually around 475-500°F or 245-260°C).

Prepare the Potatoes:
- In a saucepan, combine the thinly sliced potatoes, heavy cream, minced garlic, salt, and black pepper. Cook over medium heat, stirring

occasionally, until the potatoes are slightly tender and the cream has thickened.

Assemble the Pizza:
- Spread the creamy potato mixture evenly over the pizza dough, leaving a border for the crust.
- Sprinkle grated Gruyere cheese over the potato mixture.

Bake the Pizza:
- Place the pizza in the preheated oven and bake for 12-15 minutes, or until the crust is golden, and the toppings are heated through.

Finish and Garnish:
- Remove the Gratin Dauphinois Pizza from the oven. Sprinkle fresh thyme leaves over the hot pizza.

Slice and Serve:
- Allow the pizza to cool for a few minutes before slicing. Serve and enjoy your Gratin Dauphinois-inspired Pizza!

This pizza takes inspiration from the rich and creamy French dish Gratin Dauphinois, transforming it into a delightful and indulgent pizza. The layers of thinly sliced potatoes, garlic-infused cream, and melted Gruyere cheese create a luxurious and satisfying flavor profile. Bon appétit!

Tarte Tatin-inspired Apple and Goat Cheese Pizza

Ingredients:

For the Pizza Dough:

- 1 pound pizza dough (homemade or store-bought)
- Olive oil for brushing

For the Apple and Goat Cheese Topping:

- 2-3 large apples, cored and thinly sliced (use a sweet variety like Honeycrisp or Gala)
- 3 tablespoons unsalted butter
- 1/2 cup brown sugar
- 1/2 teaspoon ground cinnamon
- 4 ounces goat cheese, crumbled
- 1/4 cup chopped walnuts (optional)
- Fresh thyme leaves for garnish

Instructions:

For the Pizza Dough:

Prepare the Dough:
- Roll out the pizza dough onto a baking sheet or pizza stone. If using a pizza stone, make sure it is preheated in the oven.

Brush with Olive Oil:
- Brush the surface of the dough with olive oil.

For the Apple and Goat Cheese Topping:

Preheat the Oven:
- Preheat your oven to the highest temperature it can go (usually around 475-500°F or 245-260°C).

Caramelize the Apples:

- In a skillet, melt the butter over medium heat. Add the brown sugar and ground cinnamon, stirring until the sugar is dissolved.
- Add the thinly sliced apples to the skillet and cook until the apples are tender and caramelized, about 8-10 minutes. Remove from heat.

Assemble the Pizza:
- Arrange the caramelized apples evenly over the pizza dough, leaving a border for the crust.
- Sprinkle crumbled goat cheese over the caramelized apples.
- If using, scatter chopped walnuts over the pizza.

Bake the Pizza:
- Place the pizza in the preheated oven and bake for 12-15 minutes, or until the crust is golden, and the toppings are heated through.

Finish and Garnish:
- Remove the Apple and Goat Cheese Pizza from the oven. Sprinkle fresh thyme leaves over the hot pizza.

Slice and Serve:
- Allow the pizza to cool for a few minutes before slicing. Serve and enjoy your Tarte Tatin-inspired Apple and Goat Cheese Pizza!

This pizza combines the sweetness of caramelized apples with the tanginess of goat cheese, creating a delightful twist inspired by the classic French dessert, Tarte Tatin. The addition of thyme and walnuts adds depth and complexity to the flavors. Bon appétit!

Alsace Flammekueche Pizza

Ingredients:

For the Pizza Dough:

- 1 pound pizza dough (homemade or store-bought)
- Olive oil for brushing

For the Flammekueche Topping:

- 1 large onion, thinly sliced
- 8 ounces bacon, thinly sliced
- 1 cup crème fraîche
- 1 teaspoon caraway seeds
- Salt and black pepper to taste
- Fresh chives, chopped, for garnish

Instructions:

For the Pizza Dough:

Prepare the Dough:
- Roll out the pizza dough onto a baking sheet or pizza stone. If using a pizza stone, make sure it is preheated in the oven.

Brush with Olive Oil:
- Brush the surface of the dough with olive oil.

For the Flammekueche Topping:

Preheat the Oven:
- Preheat your oven to the highest temperature it can go (usually around 475-500°F or 245-260°C).

Sauté Onion and Bacon:
- In a skillet, cook the thinly sliced bacon until it's crispy. Remove the bacon from the skillet and set it aside.
- In the same skillet, using the bacon fat, sauté the thinly sliced onions until they are soft and golden brown.

Assemble the Pizza:

- Spread crème fraîche evenly over the pizza dough, leaving a border for the crust.
- Distribute the sautéed onions and crispy bacon over the crème fraîche.
- Sprinkle caraway seeds over the top.

Season and Bake:
- Season the pizza with salt and black pepper to taste. Place the pizza in the preheated oven and bake for 12-15 minutes, or until the crust is golden, and the toppings are heated through.

Finish and Garnish:
- Remove the Alsace Flammekueche Pizza from the oven. Sprinkle chopped fresh chives over the hot pizza.

Slice and Serve:
- Allow the pizza to cool for a few minutes before slicing. Serve and enjoy your Alsace Flammekueche-inspired Pizza!

This pizza takes inspiration from the Alsatian specialty Flammekueche, featuring a creamy base, caramelized onions, and crispy bacon. The addition of caraway seeds and fresh chives adds a distinct and delicious flavor. Bon appétit!

Salmon and Leek Quiche Pizza

Ingredients:

For the Pizza Dough:

- 1 pound pizza dough (homemade or store-bought)
- Olive oil for brushing

For the Salmon and Leek Quiche Topping:

- 1 cup cooked salmon, flaked
- 1 leek, thinly sliced
- 1 cup shredded Gruyere cheese
- 1/2 cup cream or half-and-half
- 3 large eggs
- 1 tablespoon Dijon mustard
- Salt and black pepper to taste
- Fresh dill, chopped, for garnish

Instructions:

For the Pizza Dough:

Prepare the Dough:
- Roll out the pizza dough onto a baking sheet or pizza stone. If using a pizza stone, make sure it is preheated in the oven.

Brush with Olive Oil:
- Brush the surface of the dough with olive oil.

For the Salmon and Leek Quiche Topping:

Preheat the Oven:
- Preheat your oven to the highest temperature it can go (usually around 475-500°F or 245-260°C).

Prepare the Quiche Filling:

- In a bowl, whisk together the eggs, cream (or half-and-half), Dijon mustard, salt, and black pepper until well combined.

Assemble the Pizza:
- Spread the sliced leeks evenly over the pizza dough, leaving a border for the crust.
- Distribute the flaked salmon over the leeks.
- Pour the egg and cream mixture over the top, ensuring it is evenly distributed.
- Sprinkle shredded Gruyere cheese over the entire pizza.

Bake the Pizza:
- Place the pizza in the preheated oven and bake for 12-15 minutes, or until the crust is golden, and the quiche filling is set and slightly browned on top.

Finish and Garnish:
- Remove the Salmon and Leek Quiche Pizza from the oven. Sprinkle chopped fresh dill over the hot pizza.

Slice and Serve:
- Allow the pizza to cool for a few minutes before slicing. Serve and enjoy your Salmon and Leek Quiche-inspired Pizza!

This pizza combines the flavors of a classic quiche with the richness of salmon, leeks, and Gruyere cheese. The Dijon mustard adds a hint of tanginess, and the fresh dill provides a burst of herbaceous freshness. Bon appétit!

French Blue Cheese and Pear Pizza

Ingredients:

For the Pizza Dough:

- 1 pound pizza dough (homemade or store-bought)
- Olive oil for brushing

For the Blue Cheese and Pear Topping:

- 1 cup crumbled French blue cheese (such as Roquefort or Bleu d'Auvergne)
- 2 ripe pears, thinly sliced
- 1/2 cup chopped walnuts
- 1 tablespoon honey
- 1 tablespoon balsamic glaze (optional)
- Fresh thyme leaves for garnish
- Salt and black pepper to taste

Instructions:

For the Pizza Dough:

Prepare the Dough:
- Roll out the pizza dough onto a baking sheet or pizza stone. If using a pizza stone, make sure it is preheated in the oven.

Brush with Olive Oil:
- Brush the surface of the dough with olive oil.

For the Blue Cheese and Pear Topping:

Preheat the Oven:
- Preheat your oven to the highest temperature it can go (usually around 475-500°F or 245-260°C).

Assemble the Pizza:
- Spread crumbled blue cheese evenly over the pizza dough, leaving a border for the crust.
- Arrange thinly sliced pears and chopped walnuts over the blue cheese.

Drizzle with Honey:
- Drizzle honey over the top of the pizza for added sweetness.

Season and Bake:
- Season the pizza with a pinch of salt and black pepper to taste. Place the pizza in the preheated oven and bake for 12-15 minutes, or until the crust is golden, and the toppings are heated through.

Optional Balsamic Glaze:
- If desired, drizzle balsamic glaze over the hot pizza for extra flavor.

Finish and Garnish:
- Remove the Blue Cheese and Pear Pizza from the oven. Sprinkle fresh thyme leaves over the hot pizza.

Slice and Serve:
- Allow the pizza to cool for a few minutes before slicing. Serve and enjoy your French Blue Cheese and Pear Pizza!

This pizza combines the rich and tangy flavor of French blue cheese with the sweetness of ripe pears and the crunch of walnuts. The honey and optional balsamic glaze add layers of sweetness and complexity. It's a sophisticated and delicious pizza option. Bon appétit!

Croissant Crust Breakfast Pizza

Ingredients:

For the Croissant Crust:

- 1 tube (8 ounces) refrigerated crescent roll dough

For the Breakfast Pizza Toppings:

- 4 large eggs
- 1/2 cup shredded mozzarella cheese
- 1/2 cup diced cooked ham or cooked and crumbled breakfast sausage
- 1/4 cup diced bell peppers (any color)
- 1/4 cup diced tomatoes
- 1/4 cup sliced mushrooms
- Salt and black pepper to taste
- Fresh parsley, chopped, for garnish

Instructions:

Preheat the Oven:
- Preheat your oven according to the crescent roll package instructions.

Prepare the Croissant Crust:
- Roll out the crescent roll dough onto a baking sheet, forming a crust by pressing the seams together to seal. Follow the instructions on the package for baking the crust until it's golden brown.

Cook the Eggs:
- While the crust is baking, scramble the eggs in a bowl. Cook them in a skillet over medium heat until just set.

Assemble the Pizza:
- Once the croissant crust is baked and golden, spread the scrambled eggs evenly over the crust.
- Sprinkle shredded mozzarella cheese, diced ham or sausage, diced bell peppers, diced tomatoes, and sliced mushrooms over the eggs.

Season:
- Season the pizza with salt and black pepper to taste.

Bake Again:

- Place the topped pizza back in the oven and bake for a few more minutes until the cheese is melted and bubbly.

Garnish:
- Remove the Breakfast Pizza from the oven and sprinkle chopped fresh parsley over the top.

Slice and Serve:
- Allow the pizza to cool for a few minutes before slicing. Serve and enjoy your Croissant Crust Breakfast Pizza!

This breakfast pizza features a flaky croissant crust as the base, topped with scrambled eggs, melty cheese, and a variety of savory breakfast ingredients. It's a delicious and satisfying way to start the day. Bon appétit!

Pâté and Cornichon Pizza

Ingredients:

For the Pizza Dough:

- 1 pound pizza dough (homemade or store-bought)
- Olive oil for brushing

For the Pâté and Cornichon Topping:

- 1/2 cup chicken liver pâté (store-bought or homemade)
- 1/2 cup sliced cornichons (small pickles)
- 1 cup shredded Gruyere cheese
- 1 tablespoon Dijon mustard
- Fresh parsley, chopped, for garnish
- Salt and black pepper to taste

Instructions:

For the Pizza Dough:

Prepare the Dough:
- Roll out the pizza dough onto a baking sheet or pizza stone. If using a pizza stone, make sure it is preheated in the oven.

Brush with Olive Oil:
- Brush the surface of the dough with olive oil.

For the Pâté and Cornichon Topping:

Preheat the Oven:
- Preheat your oven to the highest temperature it can go (usually around 475-500°F or 245-260°C).

Assemble the Pizza:
- Spread chicken liver pâté evenly over the pizza dough, leaving a border for the crust.
- Sprinkle shredded Gruyere cheese over the pâté.
- Arrange sliced cornichons over the cheese.

Drizzle with Dijon Mustard:
- Drizzle Dijon mustard over the top for added flavor.

Season:
- Season the pizza with a pinch of salt and black pepper to taste.

Bake the Pizza:
- Place the pizza in the preheated oven and bake for 12-15 minutes, or until the crust is golden, and the toppings are heated through.

Finish and Garnish:
- Remove the Pâté and Cornichon Pizza from the oven. Sprinkle chopped fresh parsley over the hot pizza.

Slice and Serve:
- Allow the pizza to cool for a few minutes before slicing. Serve and enjoy your Pâté and Cornichon Pizza!

This pizza takes inspiration from French cuisine, combining the rich and savory flavors of chicken liver pâté with the tanginess of cornichons. The melted Gruyere cheese and a drizzle of Dijon mustard add depth and complexity to this unique and delicious pizza. Bon appétit!

Spinach and Gruyere Soufflé Pizza

Ingredients:

For the Pizza Dough:

- 1 pound pizza dough (homemade or store-bought)
- Olive oil for brushing

For the Spinach and Gruyere Soufflé Topping:

- 1 cup fresh spinach, chopped
- 1 cup shredded Gruyere cheese
- 3 large eggs
- 1 cup whole milk
- 2 tablespoons unsalted butter
- 2 tablespoons all-purpose flour
- 1/2 teaspoon garlic powder
- 1/4 teaspoon nutmeg
- Salt and black pepper to taste
- Grated Parmesan cheese for sprinkling
- Fresh chives, chopped, for garnish

Instructions:

For the Pizza Dough:

Prepare the Dough:
- Roll out the pizza dough onto a baking sheet or pizza stone. If using a pizza stone, make sure it is preheated in the oven.

Brush with Olive Oil:
- Brush the surface of the dough with olive oil.

For the Spinach and Gruyere Soufflé Topping:

Preheat the Oven:

- Preheat your oven to the highest temperature it can go (usually around 475-500°F or 245-260°C).

Prepare the Soufflé Mixture:
- In a saucepan, melt butter over medium heat. Add flour and whisk continuously to create a roux. Cook for 1-2 minutes.
- Gradually add the milk, whisking constantly to avoid lumps. Cook until the mixture thickens.
- Remove from heat and let it cool slightly. Add the eggs one at a time, whisking well after each addition.
- Stir in garlic powder, nutmeg, salt, and black pepper. Fold in chopped spinach and shredded Gruyere cheese.

Assemble the Pizza:
- Pour the spinach and Gruyere soufflé mixture over the pizza dough, spreading it evenly and leaving a border for the crust.

Bake the Pizza:
- Place the pizza in the preheated oven and bake for 12-15 minutes, or until the crust is golden, and the soufflé topping is puffed and set.

Sprinkle with Parmesan:
- Remove the pizza from the oven and sprinkle grated Parmesan cheese over the hot soufflé.

Garnish:
- Sprinkle chopped fresh chives over the top.

Slice and Serve:
- Allow the pizza to cool for a few minutes before slicing. Serve and enjoy your Spinach and Gruyere Soufflé Pizza!

This pizza combines the light and fluffy texture of a soufflé with the earthy flavor of spinach and the nutty richness of Gruyere cheese. It's a sophisticated and delicious twist on traditional pizza. Bon appétit!

Coq au Vin Blanc Pizza

Ingredients:

For the Pizza Dough:

- 1 pound pizza dough (homemade or store-bought)
- Olive oil for brushing

For the Coq au Vin Blanc Topping:

- 2 boneless, skinless chicken breasts, cut into bite-sized pieces
- 1 cup white wine (such as Chardonnay or Sauvignon Blanc)
- 1/2 cup chicken broth
- 4 slices bacon, cooked and crumbled
- 1 cup mushrooms, sliced
- 1 small onion, thinly sliced
- 2 cloves garlic, minced
- 2 tablespoons all-purpose flour
- 2 tablespoons butter
- 1 tablespoon fresh thyme leaves
- Salt and black pepper to taste
- 1 cup shredded Gruyere cheese
- Fresh parsley, chopped, for garnish

Instructions:

For the Pizza Dough:

 Prepare the Dough:
- Roll out the pizza dough onto a baking sheet or pizza stone. If using a pizza stone, make sure it is preheated in the oven.

 Brush with Olive Oil:
- Brush the surface of the dough with olive oil.

For the Coq au Vin Blanc Topping:

 Preheat the Oven:
- Preheat your oven to the highest temperature it can go (usually around 475-500°F or 245-260°C).

Cook the Chicken:
- In a skillet, cook the chicken pieces until they are browned on all sides. Remove from the skillet and set aside.

Prepare the Sauce:
- In the same skillet, melt butter over medium heat. Add sliced mushrooms, onions, and minced garlic. Cook until the vegetables are softened.
- Sprinkle flour over the vegetables and stir well to combine.
- Gradually pour in the white wine and chicken broth, stirring continuously to avoid lumps. Cook until the sauce thickens.

Assemble the Pizza:
- Spread the coq au vin blanc sauce over the pizza dough, leaving a border for the crust.
- Distribute the cooked chicken pieces, crumbled bacon, and fresh thyme leaves over the sauce.

Season and Bake:
- Season the pizza with salt and black pepper to taste. Place the pizza in the preheated oven and bake for 12-15 minutes, or until the crust is golden, and the toppings are heated through.

Sprinkle with Gruyere:
- Remove the pizza from the oven and sprinkle shredded Gruyere cheese over the hot coq au vin blanc topping.

Garnish:
- Sprinkle chopped fresh parsley over the top.

Slice and Serve:
- Allow the pizza to cool for a few minutes before slicing. Serve and enjoy your Coq au Vin Blanc Pizza!

This pizza takes inspiration from the classic French dish Coq au Vin Blanc, featuring a white wine-based sauce with chicken, bacon, mushrooms, and onions. The addition of Gruyere cheese and fresh thyme creates a rich and savory flavor profile. Bon appétit!

French Ham and Gouda Pizza

Ingredients:

For the Pizza Dough:

- 1 pound pizza dough (homemade or store-bought)
- Olive oil for brushing

For the Ham and Gouda Topping:

- 1 cup cooked ham, thinly sliced
- 1 1/2 cups Gouda cheese, shredded
- 1/2 cup caramelized onions
- 1 tablespoon Dijon mustard
- 1 tablespoon fresh thyme leaves
- Salt and black pepper to taste
- Fresh chives, chopped, for garnish

Instructions:

For the Pizza Dough:

Prepare the Dough:
- Roll out the pizza dough onto a baking sheet or pizza stone. If using a pizza stone, make sure it is preheated in the oven.

Brush with Olive Oil:
- Brush the surface of the dough with olive oil.

For the Ham and Gouda Topping:

Preheat the Oven:
- Preheat your oven to the highest temperature it can go (usually around 475-500°F or 245-260°C).

Assemble the Pizza:
- Spread a thin layer of Dijon mustard evenly over the pizza dough, leaving a border for the crust.
- Distribute the thinly sliced ham, shredded Gouda cheese, and caramelized onions over the mustard-covered dough.
- Sprinkle fresh thyme leaves over the top.

Season:
- Season the pizza with salt and black pepper to taste.

Bake the Pizza:
- Place the pizza in the preheated oven and bake for 12-15 minutes, or until the crust is golden, and the toppings are heated through.

Garnish:
- Remove the Ham and Gouda Pizza from the oven. Sprinkle chopped fresh chives over the hot pizza.

Slice and Serve:
- Allow the pizza to cool for a few minutes before slicing. Serve and enjoy your French Ham and Gouda Pizza!

This pizza brings together the smoky and savory flavors of ham with the creamy richness of Gouda cheese. The addition of caramelized onions and Dijon mustard adds depth and complexity to create a delicious French-inspired pizza. Bon appétit!

Mushroom and Gruyere Galette Pizza

Ingredients:

For the Galette Dough:

- 1 1/4 cups all-purpose flour
- 1/4 teaspoon salt
- 1/2 cup unsalted butter, cold and cut into small pieces
- 1/4 cup ice water

For the Mushroom and Gruyere Topping:

- 2 tablespoons olive oil
- 1 pound mushrooms (such as cremini or button), sliced
- 2 cloves garlic, minced
- Salt and black pepper to taste
- 1 cup Gruyere cheese, shredded
- 2 tablespoons fresh thyme leaves
- 1 egg (for egg wash)

Instructions:

For the Galette Dough:

Prepare the Dough:
- In a food processor, combine the flour and salt. Add the cold butter pieces and pulse until the mixture resembles coarse crumbs.
- Slowly add the ice water and pulse until the dough comes together. Wrap the dough in plastic wrap and refrigerate for at least 1 hour.

For the Mushroom and Gruyere Topping:

Preheat the Oven:
- Preheat your oven to 375°F (190°C).

Sauté the Mushrooms:
- In a skillet, heat olive oil over medium heat. Add sliced mushrooms and garlic, sautéing until the mushrooms are tender. Season with salt and black pepper. Remove from heat and let it cool.

Roll out the Dough:

- On a lightly floured surface, roll out the galette dough into a round shape.

Assemble the Galette Pizza:
- Transfer the rolled-out dough to a baking sheet lined with parchment paper.
- Leaving a border, spread the sautéed mushroom mixture over the dough. Sprinkle shredded Gruyere cheese on top.
- Fold the edges of the dough over the filling, creating a rustic, free-form galette.

Brush with Egg Wash:
- Beat the egg and brush it over the edges of the galette for a golden finish.

Bake the Galette Pizza:
- Bake in the preheated oven for 25-30 minutes or until the crust is golden brown and the cheese is melted.

Garnish:
- Sprinkle fresh thyme leaves over the hot galette pizza.

Slice and Serve:
- Allow the galette to cool for a few minutes before slicing. Serve and enjoy your Mushroom and Gruyere Galette Pizza!

This pizza combines the flaky, buttery crust of a galette with the earthy flavors of sautéed mushrooms and the rich, nutty taste of Gruyere cheese. It's a deliciously rustic and elegant dish. Bon appétit!

French Lentil and Sausage Pizza

Ingredients:

For the Pizza Dough:

- 1 pound pizza dough (homemade or store-bought)
- Olive oil for brushing

For the Lentil and Sausage Topping:

- 1 cup French green lentils, cooked
- 1/2 pound French or Italian sausage, crumbled and cooked
- 1 onion, finely chopped
- 2 cloves garlic, minced
- 1 teaspoon dried thyme
- 1/2 cup tomato sauce
- Salt and black pepper to taste
- 1 cup Gruyere cheese, shredded
- Fresh parsley, chopped, for garnish

Instructions:

For the Pizza Dough:

Prepare the Dough:
- Roll out the pizza dough onto a baking sheet or pizza stone. If using a pizza stone, make sure it is preheated in the oven.

Brush with Olive Oil:
- Brush the surface of the dough with olive oil.

For the Lentil and Sausage Topping:

Preheat the Oven:
- Preheat your oven to the highest temperature it can go (usually around 475-500°F or 245-260°C).

Cook the Lentils and Sausage:
- In a skillet, cook the crumbled sausage until browned. Add chopped onions and minced garlic, cooking until softened.

- Stir in cooked green lentils, dried thyme, and tomato sauce. Season with salt and black pepper to taste. Cook for a few more minutes until the flavors meld.

Assemble the Pizza:
- Spread the lentil and sausage mixture evenly over the pizza dough, leaving a border for the crust.
- Sprinkle shredded Gruyere cheese over the lentil and sausage topping.

Bake the Pizza:
- Place the pizza in the preheated oven and bake for 12-15 minutes, or until the crust is golden, and the toppings are heated through.

Garnish:
- Remove the Lentil and Sausage Pizza from the oven. Sprinkle chopped fresh parsley over the hot pizza.

Slice and Serve:
- Allow the pizza to cool for a few minutes before slicing. Serve and enjoy your French Lentil and Sausage Pizza!

This pizza combines the heartiness of French green lentils and savory crumbled sausage, complemented by the nutty flavor of Gruyere cheese. The addition of thyme adds a touch of herbal goodness. It's a unique and satisfying pizza option. Bon appétit!

Gougères (Cheese Puffs) Pizza

Ingredients:

For the Pizza Dough:

- 1 pound pizza dough (homemade or store-bought)
- Olive oil for brushing

For the Gougères Topping:

- 1 cup Gruyere cheese, shredded
- 1/2 cup Parmesan cheese, grated
- 1/2 cup unsalted butter
- 1 cup water
- 1 cup all-purpose flour
- 4 large eggs
- 1 teaspoon Dijon mustard
- Salt and black pepper to taste
- Fresh chives, chopped, for garnish

Instructions:

For the Pizza Dough:

Prepare the Dough:
- Roll out the pizza dough onto a baking sheet or pizza stone. If using a pizza stone, make sure it is preheated in the oven.

Brush with Olive Oil:
- Brush the surface of the dough with olive oil.

For the Gougères Topping:

Preheat the Oven:
- Preheat your oven to the highest temperature it can go (usually around 475-500°F or 245-260°C).

Make the Gougères Dough:

- In a saucepan, combine butter and water. Bring to a boil. Once boiling, add the flour all at once, stirring vigorously until the mixture forms a smooth ball. Remove from heat.
- Let the mixture cool for a few minutes, then beat in the eggs one at a time until fully incorporated. Stir in Dijon mustard, Gruyere cheese, and Parmesan cheese. Season with salt and black pepper.

Assemble the Pizza:
- Spread the gougères mixture evenly over the pizza dough, leaving a border for the crust.

Bake the Pizza:
- Place the pizza in the preheated oven and bake for 12-15 minutes, or until the crust is golden, and the gougères topping is puffed and golden.

Garnish:
- Remove the Gougères Pizza from the oven. Sprinkle chopped fresh chives over the hot pizza.

Slice and Serve:
- Allow the pizza to cool for a few minutes before slicing. Serve and enjoy your Gougères Pizza!

This pizza combines the airy and cheesy goodness of gougères with the classic pizza format. The result is a delightful combination of crispy crust and cheesy puffs, making it a unique and flavorful option. Bon appétit!

Basque Piquillos and Chorizo Pizza

Ingredients:

For the Pizza Dough:

- 1 pound pizza dough (homemade or store-bought)
- Olive oil for brushing

For the Basque Piquillos and Chorizo Topping:

- 1 cup Basque piquillo peppers, drained and sliced
- 1/2 cup cured chorizo, thinly sliced
- 1 cup Manchego cheese, shredded
- 1/2 cup red onion, thinly sliced
- 2 tablespoons fresh parsley, chopped
- 1 tablespoon olive oil
- Salt and black pepper to taste

Instructions:

For the Pizza Dough:

Prepare the Dough:
- Roll out the pizza dough onto a baking sheet or pizza stone. If using a pizza stone, make sure it is preheated in the oven.

Brush with Olive Oil:
- Brush the surface of the dough with olive oil.

For the Basque Piquillos and Chorizo Topping:

Preheat the Oven:
- Preheat your oven to the highest temperature it can go (usually around 475-500°F or 245-260°C).

Assemble the Pizza:
- Arrange the sliced Basque piquillo peppers, chorizo, and red onion evenly over the pizza dough, leaving a border for the crust.
- Sprinkle shredded Manchego cheese over the toppings.

Season and Drizzle:

- Season the pizza with salt and black pepper to taste. Drizzle olive oil over the top.

Bake the Pizza:
- Place the pizza in the preheated oven and bake for 12-15 minutes, or until the crust is golden, and the toppings are heated through.

Garnish:
- Remove the Basque Piquillos and Chorizo Pizza from the oven. Sprinkle chopped fresh parsley over the hot pizza.

Slice and Serve:
- Allow the pizza to cool for a few minutes before slicing. Serve and enjoy your Basque Piquillos and Chorizo Pizza!

This pizza combines the smoky and slightly sweet flavor of Basque piquillo peppers with the bold and savory taste of cured chorizo. The addition of Manchego cheese adds a rich and nutty element, making it a delightful and unique pizza experience. Bon appétit!

French-inspired Duck Sausage Pizza

Ingredients:

For the Pizza Dough:

- 1 pound pizza dough (homemade or store-bought)
- Olive oil for brushing

For the Duck Sausage Topping:

- 1/2 pound duck sausage, cooked and sliced
- 1 cup caramelized onions
- 1 cup Gruyere cheese, shredded
- 2 tablespoons fig jam
- 1 tablespoon fresh thyme leaves
- Salt and black pepper to taste
- Arugula, for garnish (optional)

Instructions:

For the Pizza Dough:

Prepare the Dough:
- Roll out the pizza dough onto a baking sheet or pizza stone. If using a pizza stone, make sure it is preheated in the oven.

Brush with Olive Oil:
- Brush the surface of the dough with olive oil.

For the Duck Sausage Topping:

Preheat the Oven:
- Preheat your oven to the highest temperature it can go (usually around 475-500°F or 245-260°C).

Assemble the Pizza:
- Spread a thin layer of fig jam evenly over the pizza dough, leaving a border for the crust.

- Distribute the cooked and sliced duck sausage and caramelized onions over the jam-covered dough.
- Sprinkle shredded Gruyere cheese over the toppings.

Season and Bake:
- Season the pizza with salt and black pepper to taste. Place the pizza in the preheated oven and bake for 12-15 minutes, or until the crust is golden, and the toppings are heated through.

Garnish:
- Remove the Duck Sausage Pizza from the oven. Sprinkle fresh thyme leaves over the hot pizza. Optionally, top with a handful of arugula for a peppery finish.

Slice and Serve:
- Allow the pizza to cool for a few minutes before slicing. Serve and enjoy your French-inspired Duck Sausage Pizza!

This pizza combines the rich and savory flavors of duck sausage with the sweetness of fig jam and the nutty taste of Gruyere cheese. Caramelized onions add depth, and fresh thyme leaves bring a touch of herbal freshness. It's a sophisticated and delicious French twist on pizza. Bon appétit!

Comté Cheese and Potato Pizza

Ingredients:

For the Pizza Dough:

- 1 pound pizza dough (homemade or store-bought)
- Olive oil for brushing

For the Comté Cheese and Potato Topping:

- 1 large potato, thinly sliced
- 1 cup Comté cheese, shredded
- 2 tablespoons olive oil
- 2 cloves garlic, minced
- 1 tablespoon fresh rosemary, chopped
- Salt and black pepper to taste
- 1/4 cup Parmesan cheese, grated
- Arugula, for garnish (optional)

Instructions:

For the Pizza Dough:

Prepare the Dough:
- Roll out the pizza dough onto a baking sheet or pizza stone. If using a pizza stone, make sure it is preheated in the oven.

Brush with Olive Oil:
- Brush the surface of the dough with olive oil.

For the Comté Cheese and Potato Topping:

Preheat the Oven:
- Preheat your oven to the highest temperature it can go (usually around 475-500°F or 245-260°C).

Prepare the Potato Slices:
- In a bowl, toss the thinly sliced potato with olive oil, minced garlic, chopped rosemary, salt, and black pepper.

Assemble the Pizza:

- Arrange the seasoned potato slices evenly over the pizza dough, leaving a border for the crust.
- Sprinkle shredded Comté cheese over the potato slices.

Bake the Pizza:
- Place the pizza in the preheated oven and bake for 12-15 minutes, or until the crust is golden, and the potato slices are tender and golden.

Finish with Parmesan:
- Remove the pizza from the oven and sprinkle grated Parmesan cheese over the hot Comté Cheese and Potato Pizza.

Garnish:
- Optionally, top with a handful of fresh arugula for a peppery finish.

Slice and Serve:
- Allow the pizza to cool for a few minutes before slicing. Serve and savor your Comté Cheese and Potato Pizza!

This pizza highlights the creamy and nutty flavor of Comté cheese paired with the earthy goodness of roasted potato slices. The addition of garlic and rosemary enhances the overall taste, making it a delightful and sophisticated pizza. Bon appétit!

Salmon Rillettes and Cucumber Pizza

Ingredients:

For the Pizza Dough:

- 1 pound pizza dough (homemade or store-bought)
- Olive oil for brushing

For the Salmon Rillettes and Cucumber Topping:

- 1/2 pound smoked salmon, flaked
- 1/2 cup cream cheese
- 1/4 cup Greek yogurt
- 1 tablespoon fresh dill, chopped
- Zest of 1 lemon
- Salt and black pepper to taste
- 1 cucumber, thinly sliced
- Red onion, thinly sliced
- Capers, for garnish
- Fresh chives, chopped, for garnish

Instructions:

For the Pizza Dough:

Prepare the Dough:
- Roll out the pizza dough onto a baking sheet or pizza stone. If using a pizza stone, make sure it is preheated in the oven.

Brush with Olive Oil:
- Brush the surface of the dough with olive oil.

For the Salmon Rillettes and Cucumber Topping:

Preheat the Oven:
- Preheat your oven to the highest temperature it can go (usually around 475-500°F or 245-260°C).

Make the Salmon Rillettes:
- In a bowl, combine the flaked smoked salmon, cream cheese, Greek yogurt, chopped dill, lemon zest, salt, and black pepper. Mix until well combined.

Assemble the Pizza:
- Spread the salmon rillettes mixture evenly over the pizza dough, leaving a border for the crust.
- Arrange thin cucumber slices and red onion slices on top of the salmon rillettes.

Bake the Pizza:
- Place the pizza in the preheated oven and bake for 12-15 minutes, or until the crust is golden, and the toppings are heated through.

Garnish:
- Remove the Salmon Rillettes and Cucumber Pizza from the oven. Sprinkle capers and chopped fresh chives over the hot pizza.

Slice and Serve:
- Allow the pizza to cool for a few minutes before slicing. Serve and enjoy your Salmon Rillettes and Cucumber Pizza!

This pizza offers a delightful combination of creamy salmon rillettes, the crisp freshness of cucumber, and the zesty brightness of lemon and dill. It's a perfect choice for a light and elegant meal. Bon appétit!

Leek and Bacon Quiche Pizza

Ingredients:

For the Pizza Dough:

- 1 pound pizza dough (homemade or store-bought)
- Olive oil for brushing

For the Leek and Bacon Quiche Topping:

- 1 tablespoon olive oil
- 2 leeks, white and light green parts, thinly sliced
- 6 slices bacon, cooked and crumbled
- 1 cup Gruyere cheese, shredded
- 1/2 cup heavy cream
- 3 large eggs
- Salt and black pepper to taste
- Fresh thyme leaves, for garnish

Instructions:

For the Pizza Dough:

Prepare the Dough:
- Roll out the pizza dough onto a baking sheet or pizza stone. If using a pizza stone, make sure it is preheated in the oven.

Brush with Olive Oil:
- Brush the surface of the dough with olive oil.

For the Leek and Bacon Quiche Topping:

Preheat the Oven:
- Preheat your oven to the highest temperature it can go (usually around 475-500°F or 245-260°C).

Prepare the Leek and Bacon Mixture:

- In a skillet, heat olive oil over medium heat. Add sliced leeks and cook until softened, about 5 minutes.
- In a bowl, whisk together heavy cream, eggs, salt, and black pepper.

Assemble the Pizza:
- Spread the sautéed leeks evenly over the pizza dough, leaving a border for the crust.
- Sprinkle crumbled bacon over the leeks, and then distribute the shredded Gruyere cheese on top.
- Pour the cream and egg mixture evenly over the toppings.

Bake the Pizza:
- Place the pizza in the preheated oven and bake for 12-15 minutes, or until the crust is golden, and the quiche is set and slightly golden on top.

Garnish:
- Remove the Leek and Bacon Quiche Pizza from the oven. Sprinkle fresh thyme leaves over the hot pizza.

Slice and Serve:
- Allow the pizza to cool for a few minutes before slicing. Serve and enjoy your Leek and Bacon Quiche Pizza!

This pizza combines the flavors of a classic quiche with the convenience of a pizza. The leeks and bacon add savory goodness, while Gruyere cheese provides a rich and nutty taste. It's a perfect choice for brunch or a cozy dinner. Bon appétit!

Pissaladière with Anchovies and Olives Pizza

Ingredients:

For the Pizza Dough:

- 1 pound pizza dough (homemade or store-bought)
- Olive oil for brushing

For the Pissaladière Topping:

- 2 tablespoons olive oil
- 4 large onions, thinly sliced
- 2 cloves garlic, minced
- 1 teaspoon dried thyme
- Salt and black pepper to taste
- 1/2 cup black olives, pitted and sliced
- 1/2 cup anchovy fillets in oil, drained
- Fresh rosemary, chopped, for garnish

Instructions:

For the Pizza Dough:

Prepare the Dough:
- Roll out the pizza dough onto a baking sheet or pizza stone. If using a pizza stone, make sure it is preheated in the oven.

Brush with Olive Oil:
- Brush the surface of the dough with olive oil.

For the Pissaladière Topping:

Preheat the Oven:
- Preheat your oven to the highest temperature it can go (usually around 475-500°F or 245-260°C).

Caramelize the Onions:

- In a large skillet, heat olive oil over medium heat. Add thinly sliced onions and cook, stirring occasionally, until the onions are golden brown and caramelized.
- Add minced garlic, dried thyme, salt, and black pepper. Cook for an additional 2-3 minutes. Remove from heat and let it cool.

Assemble the Pizza:
- Spread the caramelized onion mixture evenly over the pizza dough, leaving a border for the crust.
- Arrange sliced black olives and anchovy fillets over the onion topping.

Bake the Pizza:
- Place the pizza in the preheated oven and bake for 12-15 minutes, or until the crust is golden, and the toppings are heated through.

Garnish:
- Remove the Pissaladière with Anchovies and Olives Pizza from the oven. Sprinkle chopped fresh rosemary over the hot pizza.

Slice and Serve:
- Allow the pizza to cool for a few minutes before slicing. Serve and enjoy your Pissaladière with Anchovies and Olives Pizza!

This pizza showcases the flavors of the classic French pissaladière, with sweet and savory caramelized onions, briny anchovies, and flavorful olives. The addition of rosemary adds a fragrant touch, creating a delightful and sophisticated pizza. Bon appétit!

French Herb and Goat Cheese Pizza

Ingredients:

For the Pizza Dough:

- 1 pound pizza dough (homemade or store-bought)
- Olive oil for brushing

For the French Herb and Goat Cheese Topping:

- 4 ounces goat cheese, crumbled
- 2 tablespoons fresh chives, chopped
- 2 tablespoons fresh parsley, chopped
- 1 tablespoon fresh tarragon, chopped
- 1 tablespoon fresh thyme leaves
- 1 tablespoon fresh rosemary, chopped
- 2 cloves garlic, minced
- Zest of 1 lemon
- Salt and black pepper to taste
- 1/4 cup Parmesan cheese, grated (optional)

Instructions:

For the Pizza Dough:

Prepare the Dough:
- Roll out the pizza dough onto a baking sheet or pizza stone. If using a pizza stone, make sure it is preheated in the oven.

Brush with Olive Oil:
- Brush the surface of the dough with olive oil.

For the French Herb and Goat Cheese Topping:

Preheat the Oven:
- Preheat your oven to the highest temperature it can go (usually around 475-500°F or 245-260°C).

Assemble the Pizza:
- Spread the crumbled goat cheese evenly over the pizza dough, leaving a border for the crust.

- In a bowl, mix together chopped chives, parsley, tarragon, thyme leaves, rosemary, minced garlic, lemon zest, salt, and black pepper.
- Sprinkle the herb mixture over the goat cheese on the pizza.

Optional Parmesan Topping:
- If desired, sprinkle grated Parmesan cheese over the pizza for an extra layer of flavor.

Bake the Pizza:
- Place the pizza in the preheated oven and bake for 12-15 minutes, or until the crust is golden, and the toppings are heated through.

Slice and Serve:
- Allow the pizza to cool for a few minutes before slicing. Serve and enjoy your French Herb and Goat Cheese Pizza!

This pizza celebrates the vibrant flavors of fresh herbs combined with the creamy and tangy taste of goat cheese. The addition of lemon zest adds a bright citrusy note, creating a pizza that is both fresh and flavorful. Bon appétit!

Alsace Onion and Bacon Tart Pizza

Ingredients:

For the Pizza Dough:

- 1 pound pizza dough (homemade or store-bought)
- Olive oil for brushing

For the Alsace Onion and Bacon Tart Topping:

- 2 large onions, thinly sliced
- 4 slices of bacon, chopped
- 1 tablespoon unsalted butter
- 1 tablespoon all-purpose flour
- 1/2 cup heavy cream
- 1 teaspoon Dijon mustard
- Salt and black pepper to taste
- 1 cup Gruyere cheese, shredded
- Fresh thyme leaves for garnish

Instructions:

For the Pizza Dough:

Prepare the Dough:
- Roll out the pizza dough onto a baking sheet or pizza stone. If using a pizza stone, make sure it is preheated in the oven.

Brush with Olive Oil:
- Brush the surface of the dough with olive oil.

For the Alsace Onion and Bacon Tart Topping:

Preheat the Oven:
- Preheat your oven to the highest temperature it can go (usually around 475-500°F or 245-260°C).

Caramelize the Onions:

- In a skillet, melt butter over medium heat. Add thinly sliced onions and cook, stirring occasionally, until the onions are soft and caramelized.
- Add chopped bacon to the skillet and cook until the bacon is crispy. Remove excess grease.

Make the Cream Sauce:
- Sprinkle flour over the onion and bacon mixture and stir to combine. Cook for a minute to remove the raw flour taste.
- Gradually pour in the heavy cream, stirring continuously to avoid lumps. Stir in Dijon mustard. Cook until the mixture thickens. Season with salt and black pepper.

Assemble the Pizza:
- Spread the onion and bacon cream sauce evenly over the pizza dough, leaving a border for the crust.
- Sprinkle shredded Gruyere cheese over the cream sauce.

Bake the Pizza:
- Place the pizza in the preheated oven and bake for 12-15 minutes, or until the crust is golden, and the toppings are bubbly and golden.

Garnish:
- Remove the Alsace Onion and Bacon Tart Pizza from the oven. Sprinkle fresh thyme leaves over the hot pizza.

Slice and Serve:
- Allow the pizza to cool for a few minutes before slicing. Serve and enjoy your Alsace Onion and Bacon Tart Pizza!

This pizza combines the rich and savory flavors of caramelized onions and bacon with the creamy goodness of Gruyere cheese, creating a delicious Alsace-inspired tart on a pizza crust. Bon appétit!

Chicken Liver Pâté and Fig Pizza

Ingredients:

For the Pizza Dough:

- 1 pound pizza dough (homemade or store-bought)
- Olive oil for brushing

For the Chicken Liver Pâté and Fig Topping:

- 1/2 cup chicken liver pâté
- 6-8 fresh figs, sliced
- 1/2 cup goat cheese, crumbled
- 1/4 cup caramelized onions
- Fresh thyme leaves for garnish
- Balsamic glaze for drizzling

Instructions:

For the Pizza Dough:

Prepare the Dough:
- Roll out the pizza dough onto a baking sheet or pizza stone. If using a pizza stone, make sure it is preheated in the oven.

Brush with Olive Oil:
- Brush the surface of the dough with olive oil.

For the Chicken Liver Pâté and Fig Topping:

Preheat the Oven:
- Preheat your oven to the highest temperature it can go (usually around 475-500°F or 245-260°C).

Assemble the Pizza:
- Spread the chicken liver pâté evenly over the pizza dough, leaving a border for the crust.
- Arrange sliced fresh figs and crumbled goat cheese over the pâté.
- Distribute caramelized onions over the figs and goat cheese.

Bake the Pizza:

- Place the pizza in the preheated oven and bake for 12-15 minutes, or until the crust is golden, and the toppings are heated through.

Garnish:
- Remove the Chicken Liver Pâté and Fig Pizza from the oven. Sprinkle fresh thyme leaves over the hot pizza.

Drizzle with Balsamic Glaze:
- Drizzle balsamic glaze over the pizza for an extra burst of flavor.

Slice and Serve:
- Allow the pizza to cool for a few minutes before slicing. Serve and enjoy your Chicken Liver Pâté and Fig Pizza!

This pizza offers a delightful combination of rich and creamy chicken liver pâté, sweet and juicy figs, tangy goat cheese, and the depth of flavor from caramelized onions. The balsamic glaze adds a touch of sweetness and acidity, creating a sophisticated and indulgent pizza experience. Bon appétit!

French Ratatouille and Goat Cheese Pizza

Ingredients:

For the Pizza Dough:

- 1 pound pizza dough (homemade or store-bought)
- Olive oil for brushing

For the Ratatouille and Goat Cheese Topping:

- 1 cup eggplant, diced
- 1 cup zucchini, diced
- 1 cup bell peppers (red and yellow), diced
- 1 cup cherry tomatoes, halved
- 1/2 cup red onion, thinly sliced
- 2 cloves garlic, minced
- 3 tablespoons olive oil
- 1 teaspoon dried thyme
- 1 teaspoon dried oregano
- Salt and black pepper to taste
- 1/2 cup goat cheese, crumbled
- Fresh basil leaves for garnish

Instructions:

For the Pizza Dough:

Prepare the Dough:
- Roll out the pizza dough onto a baking sheet or pizza stone. If using a pizza stone, make sure it is preheated in the oven.

Brush with Olive Oil:
- Brush the surface of the dough with olive oil.

For the Ratatouille and Goat Cheese Topping:

Preheat the Oven:

- Preheat your oven to the highest temperature it can go (usually around 475-500°F or 245-260°C).

Prepare the Ratatouille:
- In a large skillet, heat olive oil over medium heat. Add minced garlic and sauté until fragrant.
- Add diced eggplant, zucchini, bell peppers, cherry tomatoes, and red onion to the skillet. Cook until the vegetables are tender but still have a slight bite.
- Season with dried thyme, dried oregano, salt, and black pepper. Stir well to combine. Remove from heat.

Assemble the Pizza:
- Spread the prepared ratatouille mixture evenly over the pizza dough, leaving a border for the crust.
- Crumble goat cheese over the ratatouille.

Bake the Pizza:
- Place the pizza in the preheated oven and bake for 12-15 minutes, or until the crust is golden, and the toppings are heated through.

Garnish:
- Remove the Ratatouille and Goat Cheese Pizza from the oven. Sprinkle fresh basil leaves over the hot pizza.

Slice and Serve:
- Allow the pizza to cool for a few minutes before slicing. Serve and enjoy your French Ratatouille and Goat Cheese Pizza!

This pizza showcases the classic French ratatouille with a twist, combining the vibrant flavors of assorted vegetables with the creamy richness of goat cheese. It's a delightful and colorful pizza that captures the essence of French cuisine. Bon appétit!

Blue Cheese and Caramelized Pear Pizza

Ingredients:

For the Pizza Dough:

- 1 pound pizza dough (homemade or store-bought)
- Olive oil for brushing

For the Blue Cheese and Caramelized Pear Topping:

- 2 ripe pears, thinly sliced
- 1 tablespoon unsalted butter
- 2 tablespoons brown sugar
- 1 cup blue cheese, crumbled
- 1/2 cup walnuts, chopped
- Honey for drizzling
- Fresh arugula for garnish

Instructions:

For the Pizza Dough:

Prepare the Dough:
- Roll out the pizza dough onto a baking sheet or pizza stone. If using a pizza stone, make sure it is preheated in the oven.

Brush with Olive Oil:
- Brush the surface of the dough with olive oil.

For the Blue Cheese and Caramelized Pear Topping:

Preheat the Oven:
- Preheat your oven to the highest temperature it can go (usually around 475-500°F or 245-260°C).

Caramelize the Pears:

- In a skillet, melt butter over medium heat. Add thinly sliced pears and brown sugar. Cook until the pears are caramelized and golden brown. Remove from heat and set aside.

Assemble the Pizza:
- Spread the caramelized pear slices evenly over the pizza dough, leaving a border for the crust.
- Sprinkle crumbled blue cheese and chopped walnuts over the pears.

Bake the Pizza:
- Place the pizza in the preheated oven and bake for 12-15 minutes, or until the crust is golden, and the cheese is melted and bubbly.

Drizzle with Honey:
- Remove the Blue Cheese and Caramelized Pear Pizza from the oven. Drizzle honey over the hot pizza.

Garnish:
- Top the pizza with fresh arugula for a peppery finish.

Slice and Serve:
- Allow the pizza to cool for a few minutes before slicing. Serve and enjoy your Blue Cheese and Caramelized Pear Pizza!

This pizza combines the sweet and caramelized goodness of pears with the bold and tangy flavor of blue cheese, creating a perfect balance of sweetness and savory richness. The addition of walnuts and honey adds extra texture and depth of flavor. Bon appétit!

French Tarragon Chicken Pizza

Ingredients:

For the Pizza Dough:

- 1 pound pizza dough (homemade or store-bought)
- Olive oil for brushing

For the French Tarragon Chicken Topping:

- 1 cup cooked chicken, shredded or diced
- 1 tablespoon olive oil
- 1 small onion, thinly sliced
- 2 cloves garlic, minced
- 1/2 cup cremini mushrooms, sliced
- 2 tablespoons fresh tarragon, chopped
- Salt and black pepper to taste
- 1/2 cup Gruyere cheese, shredded
- 1/2 cup mozzarella cheese, shredded
- 2 tablespoons Parmesan cheese, grated
- Fresh tarragon leaves for garnish

Instructions:

For the Pizza Dough:

Prepare the Dough:
- Roll out the pizza dough onto a baking sheet or pizza stone. If using a pizza stone, make sure it is preheated in the oven.

Brush with Olive Oil:
- Brush the surface of the dough with olive oil.

For the French Tarragon Chicken Topping:

Preheat the Oven:

- Preheat your oven to the highest temperature it can go (usually around 475-500°F or 245-260°C).

Sauté the Chicken and Vegetables:
- In a skillet, heat olive oil over medium heat. Add sliced onions, minced garlic, and sliced mushrooms. Sauté until the vegetables are soft and the onions are caramelized.
- Add cooked chicken to the skillet. Stir in fresh chopped tarragon. Season with salt and black pepper. Cook for an additional 2-3 minutes.

Assemble the Pizza:
- Spread the chicken and vegetable mixture evenly over the pizza dough, leaving a border for the crust.
- Sprinkle a combination of Gruyere, mozzarella, and Parmesan cheeses over the chicken and vegetables.

Bake the Pizza:
- Place the pizza in the preheated oven and bake for 12-15 minutes, or until the crust is golden, and the cheese is melted and bubbly.

Garnish:
- Remove the French Tarragon Chicken Pizza from the oven. Sprinkle fresh tarragon leaves over the hot pizza.

Slice and Serve:
- Allow the pizza to cool for a few minutes before slicing. Serve and enjoy your French Tarragon Chicken Pizza!

This pizza showcases the aromatic and slightly licorice-like flavor of tarragon, complemented by the savory combination of chicken, mushrooms, and caramelized onions. The blend of cheeses adds a rich and gooey texture to this French-inspired pizza. Bon appétit!

Garlic Butter Escargot and Mushroom Pizza

Ingredients:

For the Pizza Dough:

- 1 pound pizza dough (homemade or store-bought)
- Olive oil for brushing

For the Garlic Butter Escargot and Mushroom Topping:

- 1 can (7.5 ounces) escargot, drained
- 2 tablespoons unsalted butter
- 4 cloves garlic, minced
- 1 cup mushrooms, sliced
- Salt and black pepper to taste
- 1 tablespoon fresh parsley, chopped
- 1 cup mozzarella cheese, shredded
- Grated Parmesan cheese for sprinkling

Instructions:

For the Pizza Dough:

Prepare the Dough:
- Roll out the pizza dough onto a baking sheet or pizza stone. If using a pizza stone, make sure it is preheated in the oven.

Brush with Olive Oil:
- Brush the surface of the dough with olive oil.

For the Garlic Butter Escargot and Mushroom Topping:

Preheat the Oven:
- Preheat your oven to the highest temperature it can go (usually around 475-500°F or 245-260°C).

Prepare the Garlic Butter:
- In a small saucepan, melt the unsalted butter over medium heat. Add minced garlic and cook for 1-2 minutes until fragrant.

Cook the Escargot and Mushrooms:

- Add the drained escargot and sliced mushrooms to the garlic butter. Season with salt and black pepper. Cook for 3-4 minutes until the mushrooms are tender and the escargot are heated through.

Assemble the Pizza:
- Spread the escargot and mushroom mixture evenly over the pizza dough, leaving a border for the crust.
- Sprinkle shredded mozzarella cheese over the escargot and mushrooms.

Bake the Pizza:
- Place the pizza in the preheated oven and bake for 12-15 minutes, or until the crust is golden, and the cheese is melted and bubbly.

Garnish:
- Remove the Garlic Butter Escargot and Mushroom Pizza from the oven. Sprinkle chopped fresh parsley and grated Parmesan cheese over the hot pizza.

Slice and Serve:
- Allow the pizza to cool for a few minutes before slicing. Serve and enjoy your Garlic Butter Escargot and Mushroom Pizza!

This pizza offers a sophisticated blend of flavors with the garlic-infused butter, tender escargot, earthy mushrooms, and the richness of melted cheese. It's a unique and indulgent pizza experience. Bon appétit!

Caramelized Shallot and Thyme Pizza

Ingredients:

For the Pizza Dough:

- 1 pound pizza dough (homemade or store-bought)
- Olive oil for brushing

For the Caramelized Shallot and Thyme Topping:

- 4 large shallots, thinly sliced
- 2 tablespoons unsalted butter
- 1 tablespoon olive oil
- 1 teaspoon brown sugar
- 1 teaspoon balsamic vinegar
- Fresh thyme leaves, chopped
- Salt and black pepper to taste
- 1 cup Gruyere cheese, shredded
- 1/2 cup Parmesan cheese, grated

Instructions:

For the Pizza Dough:

Prepare the Dough:
- Roll out the pizza dough onto a baking sheet or pizza stone. If using a pizza stone, make sure it is preheated in the oven.

Brush with Olive Oil:
- Brush the surface of the dough with olive oil.

For the Caramelized Shallot and Thyme Topping:

Preheat the Oven:
- Preheat your oven to the highest temperature it can go (usually around 475-500°F or 245-260°C).

Caramelize the Shallots:
- In a skillet, melt butter and olive oil over medium heat. Add thinly sliced shallots and cook, stirring occasionally, until the shallots are soft and golden brown.

- Sprinkle brown sugar over the shallots and stir. Cook for an additional 1-2 minutes.
- Add balsamic vinegar, fresh thyme leaves, salt, and black pepper. Stir well and cook for another 2-3 minutes until the shallots are caramelized. Remove from heat.

Assemble the Pizza:
- Spread the caramelized shallot and thyme mixture evenly over the pizza dough, leaving a border for the crust.
- Sprinkle shredded Gruyere cheese over the shallot and thyme mixture.

Bake the Pizza:
- Place the pizza in the preheated oven and bake for 12-15 minutes, or until the crust is golden, and the cheese is melted and bubbly.

Sprinkle with Parmesan:
- Remove the Caramelized Shallot and Thyme Pizza from the oven. Sprinkle grated Parmesan cheese over the hot pizza.

Slice and Serve:
- Allow the pizza to cool for a few minutes before slicing. Serve and enjoy your Caramelized Shallot and Thyme Pizza!

This pizza offers a sweet and savory combination with the rich, caramelized shallots and the aromatic thyme. The Gruyere and Parmesan cheeses add a deliciously gooey and flavorful finish. Bon appétit!

French Raclette and Potato Pizza

Ingredients:

For the Pizza Dough:

- 1 pound pizza dough (homemade or store-bought)
- Olive oil for brushing

For the Raclette and Potato Topping:

- 1 cup raclette cheese, shredded
- 2 medium-sized potatoes, thinly sliced
- 1 tablespoon olive oil
- 2 cloves garlic, minced
- 1 tablespoon fresh rosemary, chopped
- Salt and black pepper to taste
- 1/2 cup caramelized onions (optional)
- Fresh parsley for garnish

Instructions:

For the Pizza Dough:

Prepare the Dough:
- Roll out the pizza dough onto a baking sheet or pizza stone. If using a pizza stone, make sure it is preheated in the oven.

Brush with Olive Oil:
- Brush the surface of the dough with olive oil.

For the Raclette and Potato Topping:

Preheat the Oven:
- Preheat your oven to the highest temperature it can go (usually around 475-500°F or 245-260°C).

Cook the Potatoes:
- In a skillet, heat olive oil over medium heat. Add thinly sliced potatoes and minced garlic. Cook until the potatoes are slightly golden and tender. Season with salt and black pepper.

Assemble the Pizza:

- Spread the cooked potato slices evenly over the pizza dough, leaving a border for the crust.
- Sprinkle shredded raclette cheese over the potatoes.
- Optionally, distribute caramelized onions over the cheese.
- Sprinkle chopped fresh rosemary over the top.

Bake the Pizza:
- Place the pizza in the preheated oven and bake for 12-15 minutes, or until the crust is golden, and the cheese is melted and bubbly.

Garnish:
- Remove the Raclette and Potato Pizza from the oven. Sprinkle fresh parsley over the hot pizza.

Slice and Serve:
- Allow the pizza to cool for a few minutes before slicing. Serve and enjoy your French Raclette and Potato Pizza!

This pizza combines the rich and creamy flavors of raclette cheese with the earthiness of thinly sliced potatoes, creating a comforting and indulgent dish. The addition of garlic, rosemary, and caramelized onions (if desired) enhances the overall depth of flavor. Bon appétit!

Spinach and Roquefort Cheese Pizza

Ingredients:

For the Pizza Dough:

- 1 pound pizza dough (homemade or store-bought)
- Olive oil for brushing

For the Spinach and Roquefort Cheese Topping:

- 2 cups fresh spinach, washed and chopped
- 1 tablespoon olive oil
- 2 cloves garlic, minced
- 1 cup Roquefort cheese, crumbled
- Salt and black pepper to taste
- Red pepper flakes (optional for heat)
- 1/2 cup walnuts, chopped
- Fresh thyme leaves for garnish

Instructions:

For the Pizza Dough:

Prepare the Dough:
- Roll out the pizza dough onto a baking sheet or pizza stone. If using a pizza stone, make sure it is preheated in the oven.

Brush with Olive Oil:
- Brush the surface of the dough with olive oil.

For the Spinach and Roquefort Cheese Topping:

Preheat the Oven:
- Preheat your oven to the highest temperature it can go (usually around 475-500°F or 245-260°C).

Sauté the Spinach:

- In a skillet, heat olive oil over medium heat. Add minced garlic and sauté until fragrant.
- Add chopped spinach to the skillet and cook until wilted. Season with salt, black pepper, and red pepper flakes if desired. Remove from heat.

Assemble the Pizza:
- Spread the sautéed spinach evenly over the pizza dough, leaving a border for the crust.
- Sprinkle crumbled Roquefort cheese over the spinach.
- Distribute chopped walnuts over the cheese.

Bake the Pizza:
- Place the pizza in the preheated oven and bake for 12-15 minutes, or until the crust is golden, and the cheese is melted and bubbly.

Garnish:
- Remove the Spinach and Roquefort Cheese Pizza from the oven. Sprinkle fresh thyme leaves over the hot pizza.

Slice and Serve:
- Allow the pizza to cool for a few minutes before slicing. Serve and enjoy your Spinach and Roquefort Cheese Pizza!

This pizza offers a delightful combination of the earthy spinach, tangy Roquefort cheese, and the crunchy texture of walnuts. It's a gourmet pizza with a burst of flavors that will surely be a hit! Bon appétit!

Alsace Bacon and Onion Flan Pizza

Ingredients:

For the Pizza Dough:

- 1 pound pizza dough (homemade or store-bought)
- Olive oil for brushing

For the Bacon and Onion Flan Topping:

- 1 cup bacon, diced
- 1 large onion, thinly sliced
- 2 tablespoons unsalted butter
- 3 eggs
- 1 cup heavy cream
- Salt and black pepper to taste
- 1/2 teaspoon nutmeg (optional)
- 1 cup Gruyere cheese, shredded
- Chives or green onions for garnish

Instructions:

For the Pizza Dough:

Prepare the Dough:
- Roll out the pizza dough onto a baking sheet or pizza stone. If using a pizza stone, make sure it is preheated in the oven.

Brush with Olive Oil:
- Brush the surface of the dough with olive oil.

For the Bacon and Onion Flan Topping:

Preheat the Oven:
- Preheat your oven to the highest temperature it can go (usually around 475-500°F or 245-260°C).

Cook the Bacon and Onions:

- In a skillet, melt butter over medium heat. Add diced bacon and cook until crispy. Remove excess grease.
- Add thinly sliced onions to the skillet and cook until soft and caramelized. Remove from heat.

Prepare the Flan Mixture:
- In a bowl, whisk together eggs, heavy cream, salt, black pepper, and nutmeg (if using).

Assemble the Pizza:
- Spread the bacon and onion mixture evenly over the pizza dough, leaving a border for the crust.
- Pour the flan mixture over the bacon and onions.
- Sprinkle shredded Gruyere cheese over the top.

Bake the Pizza:
- Place the pizza in the preheated oven and bake for 12-15 minutes, or until the crust is golden, and the flan is set and slightly golden.

Garnish:
- Remove the Alsace Bacon and Onion Flan Pizza from the oven. Sprinkle chopped chives or green onions over the hot pizza.

Slice and Serve:
- Allow the pizza to cool for a few minutes before slicing. Serve and enjoy your Alsace Bacon and Onion Flan Pizza!

This pizza combines the rich and savory flavors of bacon and caramelized onions with the creamy texture of the flan mixture. The Gruyere cheese adds a delightful nuttiness, and the chives or green onions provide a fresh finish. Bon appétit!

www.ingramcontent.com/pod-product-compliance
Lightning Source LLC
LaVergne TN
LVHW062046070526
838201LV00080B/1987